Against Art and Artists

Against Art and Artists

Jean Gimpel

Polygon
EDINBURGH

© Jean Gimpel 1991 (revised British edition)

© Editions du Seuil 1968
© Editions Universitaires 1991 (revised edition)

This edition published by Polygon
22 George Square, Edinburgh

Set in Linotron Sabon
by Koinonia Ltd, Bury
printed and bound in
Great Britain by Redwood Press,
Melksham, Wiltshire

British Library Cataloguing
in Publication Data
Gimpel, Jean *1918-*
Against art and artists, - Rev. ed
I. Title
701.18

ISBN 0 7486 6123 9

Contents

Acknowledgements

The author wishes to express his gratitude to Mr Christopher Ligota, Mr Geoffrey Strachan and Ms Robyn Marsack for their help in the preparation of the English language editions of this book.

He is also grateful to the following for their permission to quote material in copyright: John Rewald, for passages from *Cézanne, sa vie, son oeuvre, son amitié pour Zola*; Editions Gallimard, for the extract from *La France Byzantine*; Collins Publishers, for material from *Renoir My Father*; Librairie Plon, for the passage from *D'un réalisme sans rivages*; and *The Times Literary Supplement*.

Foreword

George Moore, in his *Confessions of a Young Man*, asked rhetorically why he should care that a thousand Israelites died in the building of the pyramids, or that a young girl who was the model for Ingres' *La Source* later died of syphilis, provided that he had these beautiful works to admire. This may not be historically accurate, and Moore may not have been as callous and cynical as he sounds: no matter. He expresses an attitude to art for its own sake – *art pour l'art* – of a morally revolting, if extreme form. It is this attitude to art, among others, to which Jean Gimpel objects.

This is essentially a book about the morality of art: the morality of artistic production, of the uses – mainly commercial – to which art is put, and the moral role of the artist. It is a polemical book, as its original title clearly indicates, although the careful historical research that has gone into it may give it the appearance of a sober contribution to the history of art. It is that, too, but that is not its primary purpose. Moreover, as art history it is unusual in that it is rarely concerned with aesthetics.

The present book arose out of another – non-polemical and uncontroversial – the much-admired *Cathedral Builders (Les Bâtisseurs des cathédrals)*, the cathedrals in question being mainly French Gothic. As the title implies, Gimpel was concerned less with the cathedrals themselves as architectural objects or with their designers than with the masons who actually built them, their working conditions, rates of pay and so forth. He was also concerned with the business of financing such vast projects, and why communities should devote so much of their resources to apparent extravaganzas. With his tendency to theorise and extrapolate, Gimpel compared this building activity to the construction of skyscrapers in the United States.

What attracted Gimpel to the Middle Ages may not have been clear to him at first. What was clear was that he had grown to dislike art as it had developed subsequently or, more precisely, the notion of art as a commodity. He knew this at first-hand. His father was the famous art-dealer René Gimpel, and the family retain the business (for which his wife works), calling it Gimpel Fils. Before abstract art became fashionable, Jean had bought it. Then in 1948 he had a sudden, or perhaps not so sudden, conversion – or rather, apostasy. His experiences in the French Resistance may have sharpened his vision. He realised that art had become a cult, a religion, and he lost faith in it and its claim to importance.

Jean Gimpel has no pretensions to being a moral philosopher, and he should not be judged as such. While he proposes moral arguments against artists and the art world in general, he does so by rhetorical rather than strictly logical means. If his judgements seem occasionally outrageous, if he is given to the sometime gleeful expression of personal prejudices, this need not be a flaw in his enterprise. Gimpel is sincere in his strictures. He feels passionately that over the last six hundred years or so there has been something rotten in the state of art. And who can gainsay him?

He wants to contrast the moral and economic situation in the Middle Ages with that which followed the rise of the artist in a capitalist society. In this, it is generally agreed, he has been successful. He exposes the arrogance, greed and inhumanity that surround the production of works of art with considerable scholarship and wit. In his zeal, as Tolstoy before him, he denounces many a great artist, Raphael and Michelangelo among them. But on moral not aesthetic grounds. Here I hasten to remark that, despite his concern with infrastructure, Gimpel is no Marxist. Yet it might be said, as of Tolstoy, that his account of the development of post-medieval art might give comfort and joy to socialists of any persuasion, including William Morris and his friends.

It is important to remember that this book is not a treatise but a polemic or, rather, a diatribe, and as such very subjective. Yet it says openly what many people have known or felt but have not dared to say, for fear of tarnishing the sacred image of Art, and this makes it a serious book. For anyone interested in art in its wider context – the place of art and the artist in society – *Against Art and Artists* is an important book. When it first appeared, over twenty years ago, more than one reviewer suggested that it was a classic. They were right. As C. P. Snow wrote in the *Financial Times*: 'It is a harsh, abrasive case. Take it or leave it ... And yet, if you don't let your blood-pressure blur your vision, there is something here.' There is a great deal here.

Cyril Barrett
University of Warwick

1 □ Against art and artists

" 'I will not be a civil servant – never!'
All my father's attempts to inspire me with a vocation for government service by telling me stories from his own experience achieved the opposite effect. I was filled with nausea at the thought of being a prisoner in an office, no longer the master of my own time, compelled to devote my life's energy to filling in forms.

I was then only twelve ... One day it became clear to me that I would become a painter, an artist....

At first my father was almost speechless.

'A painter? An artist?'

He doubted my sanity and wondered if he had heard me correctly. But when I had finally convinced him of the seriousness of my intention he opposed it with all his might.

'An artist? No – never as long as I live!'

There the matter rested for both sides. My father had said 'no' and that, for him, was that. Whilst I obstinately refused to take 'no' for an answer."[1]

The story of this family quarrel is taken from *Mein Kampf*. The son who discovers in himself an irresistible call to become an artist is Adolf Hitler. As a young man he was to paint, write sonnets and plays, compose an opera, and take a keen interest in architecture. He was to visit museums and monuments, and read a history of architecture as well as Wagner's *The Work of Art and the Future*. He was to go without food so that he could afford the theatre and the opera. He was to refuse all regular work and live in Vienna as a bohemian.

His childhood friend, Kubizek, a musician, writes that

Hitler 'disclosed to me his intention to devote his life to art. ...
Art had entered his life at an early date. He devoted himself to
it with a youthful enthusiasm, convinced of his vocation as an
artist, leaving school and study to their grey monotony. ... For
my friend art meant even more. His intense need of absorbing
scrutiny, his terrific seriousness, his over-active mind needed a
counterpoise ... Adolf proposed to make of our home the
centre of a circle of art lovers.'[2]

To the world's cost Hitler's artistic career came to an end
when he failed his entrance examination to the Department of
painting at the Viennese Academy of Fine Arts. 'I was so
convinced of my success,' he writes, 'that the notice of my
rejection came like a bolt from the blue.'[3]

Henceforth his ambition was to be directed towards poli-
tics, but art remained a lifelong passion. In a speech to the
National Socialist Congress in Nuremberg in 1935 he sang
the praises of Art with a capital 'A'. And having occupied
Paris in 1940, he was anxious about the fate of Vermeer's
Astronomer from the Rothschild Collection.

In an article published in 1938, titled 'My Brother Hitler',
Thomas Mann recognized in Hitler with horror and indignation 'a kinship ... a brother who possessed, whether one likes
it or not ... a kind of artistic vocation. ... All the characteristics are there: the 'cussedness' and laziness ... the inability to
adapt ... the miserable existence in the lowest social and
moral bohemia ... the insatiable craving for compensation
and self-glorification. ...'[4]

'When Thomas Mann,' writes Arnold Hauser in his remarkable work *The Social History of Art,* 'shows that all
problematical, ambiguous and disreputable lives, all the ad-
venturers, swindlers and criminals, and finally even Hitler, are
spiritual relations of the artist, he formulates the most dreadful charge ever brought against art.'[5]

It should be made clear at this point that this study of the
behaviour and role of the artist is principally limited to
painters and sculptors; it does not concern architects, writers,
poets, musicians or actors in anything but a marginal way.

In the West since the Romantic period, certain types of

introvert who were incapable of fitting into the normal pattern of society have chosen to become artists. They have sought to avoid the pressures of the external world and to escape into the life of bohemia. Such people are maladjusted: what they have found in art is compensation.

The first writer to our knowledge, and one of the very few in France who ever dared to speak out against the disturbing faults of artists, is Proudhon. In 1863, he wrote: 'They are a class apart, imperious by their ideal but inferior in reason and morality. ... You can come to terms with a philosopher, a scientist, an industrial entrepreneur, a soldier, a lawyer, an economist; with anyone who calculates, reasons, combines, conjectures; but with an artist it is impossible.'[6]

Artists have a reputation for detachment from the goods of this world. They profess not to be interested in money. For the most part this is humbug. As soon as contemporary painters achieve success, past promises and debts of gratitude seem to have no further currency. They will abandon overnight, for a better contract, dealers who have served their cause over many years. The dealers who drive the hardest bargains are often the artist themselves. This behaviour results from their firm conviction of belonging to a superior order of beings. They look upon themselves as the high priests or demi-gods of art. They are not accountable to simple mortals. To be an artist is to fulfil one's destiny. It is a vocation, not a profession.

Our researches into the working conditions of the cathedral builders[7] showed us that to be a painter or a sculptor in the Middle Ages was a profession and not a vocation. This raised the question of how the metamorphosis came about, how it was that a workman came to be transmuted into an artist. Hence this book.

Although the idea of the artist emerged at the end of the fifteenth century in Florence, the word used in its modern sense in contrast to 'workman' and 'craftsman' does not appear until the middle of the eighteenth century. In the Middle Ages all those who worked with their hands, men of the Mechanical Arts, amongst them painters and sculptors, were simply regarded as 'workmen'. The word *ouvrier* (workman) exists in Old French and appears in the thirteenth-century statutes of Etienne Boileau, spelled variously as *'ovrier'*, *'ouvroier'*, *'houvrier'*, according to the scribe. In the fifteenth century, at the wedding of Charles the Bold, the term still designates painters and sculptors in the same way as other manual professions: 'Paiemens fais par ledit Fastret tant aux maistres peintres, tailleurs d'ymages, charpentiers et autres ouvriers.'[8]

In sixteenth-century France the word *artisan*, borrowed from the Italian *artigiano*, tends to replace *ouvrier*, without, however, eliminating it entirely. Montaigne says: 'Il sera a l'advanture excusable a un peintre ou aultre artisan ... de se travailler pour acquérir nom par ses ouvrages.'[9] And Henri III issued a decree about *'artisans et gens de mestier'*.[10] *Artisan* had not, at this stage, acquired the patronizing sense of 'mere craftsman' that it has today.

The word *artiste,* on the other hand, taken from the Latin *artista*, a medieval neologism formed from *ars*, is attested as early as the fourteenth century. Its original meaning was member of a university faculty (*ars*), master or student, educated in the Liberal Arts. In sixteenth-century French it can also be used of those engaged in chemical operations. The surgeon Ambroise Paré speaks of the things 'lesquelles se proposent tous bons ouvriers et artistes en cest art (de distillation)'.[11] *Artisan* and *artiste* are treated as equivalent in the dictionary compiled by Nicot before 1600: 'Artisan ou artiste – artifex, opifex.'

In the middle of the seventeenth century painters and sculptors in France, following the example of Italy, set out to form an academy of *beaux Arts* – not yet spelled *Beaux-Arts*. They wanted to be distinguished from other manual workers in the Mechanical Arts and achieve a status comparable to that of the university *artes*, and hence of the Liberal Arts. It is at this stage that they rejected the term *artisan* – a petition of 1648 speaks of *vil sartisans* – as unworthy of them. André Félibien, one of the first theoreticians of art in France, who was commissioned in 1668 to publish the celebrated lectures of the Académie Royale de Peinture et de Sculpture, still occasionally calls painters and sculptors *artisans*. But Roger de Piles, painter, collector, and academician, in his *Abrégé de la vie des peintres*, published in 1699, does not use the word once.

Painters and sculptors adopted a more 'educated' term, *artiste*, to define their social status. But it was some time before this meaning of the word became current. Thus in the 1694 edition of the Dictionary of the French Academy, *artisan* and *artiste* still have their sixteenth-century meanings:

> *Artisan:* ouvrier dans un Art méchanique, homme de métier.
>
> *Artiste:* celuy qui travaille dans un art. Il se dit particulièrement de ceux qui font des opérations chimiques.

It is not until the edition of 1762 that we find the first modern definition of the word artist:

> *Artiste:* Celui qui travaille dans un art où le génie et la main doivent concourir. Un peintre, un architecte sont des artistes.

If the first theme of this book is the birth of the modern 'artist', the second is the birth and propagation of the cult of art. The word 'art' is derived from the Latin *ars*, but the Latin word is more all-embracing in its meaning and less charted with overtones of value than the French and English words that derive from it. In the broadest sense, *ars* refers to a characteristic mode of action or creation, and more especially to a skill acquired by study or practice. When acquired by study, this skill is contrasted with *natura* and *ingenium*; when acquired by practice, it is the opposite of *scientia*. In the latter case the contrast between the two words implies a further nuance: *ars* being less theoretical than *scientia*, is a more physical attribute; its meaning ranges from a 'way of doing' something to 'talent'.

The meaning of the word 'art' has changed in the course of centuries. It has gradually taken on a quasi-religious connotation which it did not have in the Middle Ages. Today the word carries overtones of a new Western religion, the religion of the

Beautiful or of Aesthetics. This religion has borrowed its vocabulary from the traditional religions, as a glance at our art periodicals and books on art will show.

Thus François de Hérain writes: 'Art is a religion for us artists; even those of us who have not been successful keep their faith in an ideal that has made them creative.'[12]

And Georges Mathieu: 'The artist is one of the elect, he is chosen to incarnate the sensitivity and the sufferings of the world.'[13]

Claude Lévi-Strauss says in an interview: 'When I used to go on Thursday mornings on my pilgrimage to the rue de la Boétie, what I awaited from Picasso's picture ... was nothing less than a metaphysical perception.'[14]

Claude Rivière writing on Fontana: 'Thus, aspiring to the infinite absolute, Fontana's world becomes the revelation of that same Redemption which is promised us in Easter week.'[15]

Pierre Restany, on Yves Klein: 'The Promethean temptation takes shape: at the risk of defying the gods Yves Klein competes with Moses, he presents us with the cosmogony of modern times.'[16]

Pierre Cabanne, on Picasso: 'This being outside time ... this providential man ... this demiurge ... this incarnation of his century with his implacable gospel ... not for nothing is his farm at Mougins called Notre Dame de Vie.'[17]

And this title of an article on Lapoujade: 'Abstract painters are heretics.'

But as soon as the attempt is made to define art or beauty it becomes clear that it is as difficult a task as that of discovering the nature of God. And aestheticians, like theologians, frequently offer definitions that are contradictory.

The fanaticism of the disciples of art can even stretch as far as considering the bombing of Guernica without horror because it gave Picasso the opportunity to paint an immortal masterpiece. The dead are forgotten; the masterpieces remain.

This religion, which was professed by a minority at first, has now been adopted by most intellectuals in the West. It has also been adopted by capitalism, which has integrated art into its economic system. The country in which art flourishes the most today is the United States. Since the Federal Government introduced tax-relief laws to favour its propagation, there have been mass conversions of the citizens to this religion, which allows them to increase their wealth as well as communing in artistic fervour.

The fascination exercised by this creed is so powerful that in 1963, an official theorist of the French Communist Party, a member of the Central Committee, Roger Garaudy, became a convert to what he had hitherto abominated as capitalist and decadent. With the blessing of the Party he published a book called *D'un réalisme sans rivages*. The preface is by Louis Aragon, who hails it as an 'event ... the start of an active meditation in which art contributes to the transformation of the world'. In his book Garaudy celebrates what he once reviled: Picasso, Saint-John Perse, Kafka.

In terms that medieval hagiographers would not have disowned, Garaudy praises the almost supernatural powers of Picasso:

> He bears the world in himself ... what he has captured is not its incidentals but its basic laws. And he has shown the possibility of creating another world governed by other laws ... the course of the species and the currents of our time burst forth in him but in him they take on a cosmic or historical meaning only because he has given them form ... he has harnessed dreams to serve the future and lent the mythical power of the gods to the hands, the eyes and the heart of man. ... He carries within himself the cultural history of mankind, he participates in the total movement of the universe. In the beginning was not Picasso but a little child prodigy.[18]

Although the Soviet Union has not given its imprimatur to Garaudy's heretial and decadent work, even in that country the doctrine of 'art for art's sake' has been making progress. Indeed, under pressure from elements that supported his theories Garaudy was allowed to reply to his critics in the Soviet review *World Literature* (no. 4, 1965). Quite a number of artists in the USSR have produced non-figurative canvasses that have nothing to do with socialist realism, and have found collectors to buy them. By the mid-1960s it was certainly not impossible to envisage an exhibition of Picasso's work being held in Moscow, work which, perhaps more than that of any other painter, expresses the decadence, not of the bourgeoisie or of capitalism – both of these are still in good health – but of the Western intelligentsia. For at the turn of the century Picasso came under the decadent influence of the literary circles of both Barcelona and Paris.

The unanimous deification of Picasso by the Western intelligentsia – it succeeded in making his name the best-known in the world, better than that of any statesman, scientist, or actor – is a disgrace to our civilization and a proof of its spiritual decline. This decline thus in some sense represents the final stage in the evolution of Western intellectual society that started in Renaissance Italy.

The civilizations of the next millennium will wonder how our society, which has contributed in so many spheres to the progress of humanity, could take so passionate an interest in problems as futile as those of art, just as we now wonder how the civilization of Byzantium in 1453 could take so passionate an interest in the sex of angels. Little or nothing is left of the poets of Alexandria and late Rome, or of the innumerable scholastic disputes of the theologians of the late Middle Ages. Little or nothing will remain of the millions of words printed in our time in books of art. The heated debates of these intellectual élites in periods of decadence, which seem at the time so decisive for the destiny of the world, turn out in the end to have been so many storms in teacups.

These periods of intellectual decadence have many characteristics in common. One finds in all of them apologies for the obscure and the enigmatic, and a passion for mystical doctrines. In all of them there is the same cult of the irrational. A love of emotion, sensation, instinct, primitivism, but at the same time a love of the refined, the precious, the rare, and the artificial. Individualism is taken to extremes and becomes the cult of the ego. But what is especially characteristic of our decadence is the place accorded to the imagination and the subconscious; the hostility to reason and logic; the contempt for science and scientific thought; the supreme importance attached to the problems of language; the fact that the letter and the word take precedence over the idea, that form dominates content.

One of the few writers in France to have dared to denounce the decadence of the French intellectual milieu is Julien Benda, author of *La Trahison des clercs*, in his book *La France byzantine*, published in 1945. The intellectuals have never forgiven him for the judgements he passed in this book and there has been something of a conspiracy of silence about his work.

> The religion of the obscure as professed by its high priests wages open war on communication ... this hymn, the culmination of all those characteristics of unintelligibility that are so sought after by religions for initiates ... the absence of any moral ideal, combined with a degree of pity for anybody who adopts one ... the perfection of form concealing the poverty of content ... hatred of democracy and a flight to mysticism intended as a revenge against a regime which claims to be based on reason ... the anti-social intention of modern aesthetics ... the wish to give their pronouncements the backing of science which they otherwise profoundly despise.[19]

Benda had asked himself in his earlier work whether 'rather than liar, forger or thief, the ultimate insult for the majority of intellectuals was not "insensitive to art"'.[20] This was in any case the hierarchy of values of many a French intellectual who, not so long ago claimed impunity for open treason on the ground that he 'had talent'.

More recently, a graduate of the Ecole Normale Supérieure and a philosopher, Jean-François Revel, in *Pourquoi des philosophes* (1957) and *La Cabale des dévots* (1962), has had the courage to denounce the Byzantinism of French philosophers:

> There is no philosophy left, only scholasticism ... and our age, which is otherwise so revolutionary, may well, as regards philosophy, strike future readers the way medieval commentators strike us. Amidst a great prolif-

eration of doctrines these commentators who believed themselves to be making new inventions all the time, were in fact using a vocabulary devoid of all meaning to exercise their sterile ingenuity on tired texts.[21]

Revel has also this judicious observation to make:

Philosophy, always ready to disparage scientists and their blinkers, has identified itself in practice with the defence of religion or of modes of thought that prepare the way for it. ... In France today the majority of intellectuals who place themselves politically on the left are intellectual reactionaries, as much by their ideas as by the manner in which they formulate and disseminate them. The few thousand votes they give to the left are of little avail for the future, or even for the present, in the face of millions of minds they give to the right, that is to say minds they prepare within their sphere of influence to accept the right.[22]

What Revel writes is true of the French intelligentsia, though not of the French bourgeoisie, which has happily freed itself since the Liberation from the decadence that was one of the principal causes of the events of 1940.

In England the *Times Literary Supplement*, praising Revel and commenting on the scholastic Byzantinism prevalent in France at the present time wrote on 4 May 1962: 'The English took a long time to realize that their economic supremacy of the last century was a theory of the past. It must be hoped that the French will not take equally long to face the possibility of their not being the intellectual leaders of the world.'

In the same year a French journalist visiting New York was surprised and somewhat irritated to discover that American intellectuals tended now to be condescending towards cultural imports from France: 'New York has created its own mythology. Greenwich Village, modelled entirely on the Bohemian parts of Paris and London, has withdrawn into itself. Its heroes, its drunks, its actors, its painters, its beatnik poets have become legendary characters who no longer need European approval or even initiation to exist and develop. They now expect Europe to come to them.'

And as though to make official this intellectual reversal, the *Financial Times* itself – whose art column is one of the most highly regarded in Great Britain – published in August 1964 an important article on the decline of Paris as a centre of the world of art under the banner headline: 'Paris – Dethroned Queen of the Arts.'

London and New York have inherited from Paris the religion of Art and the sceptre of Western decadence.

2 □ Giotto,
the first bourgeois painter

Cimabue thought he held the field
In painting, and now the cry is for Giotto,
So that the other's fame is now obscured.[1]

In these lines Dante testifies to the fame of his contemporary, Giotto. A fame which was denied in their own lifetime
to painters such as Cézanne and Van Gogh.

In 1334 the Florentine Commune appointed Giotto to a
post of high responsibility, that of chief architect of the
cathedral and of the city walls, and offered him homage on
this occasion in terms that give the lie to the old saw that a
prophet is without honour in his own country. The official
document which nominates him for this task emphasizes the
Florentines' desire that 'public works in progress or to be
undertaken in the City of Florence should be executed to the
honour and embellishment of the Commune of Florence,
which cannot conveniently be achieved unless an experienced
and celebrated man is put in charge of such works. In the
whole world, it is said, no one can be found better qualified
for these and many other matters than Master Giotto
Bondone of Florence, painter. Let him be recognized in his
own land as a great master and held in high esteem in the city
above-mentioned; let him have occasion to stay here continually, from which many will benefit by his knowledge and
learning, and no small glory will accrue to the city above-
mentioned.'[2]

After his death the Florentine storytellers Boccaccio and
Sacchetti made use of Giotto as a character in their tales;
Benvenuto da Imola, who wrote a commentary on Dante and

taught at the University of Padua, lectured to his students about the life of the painter. The Florentine historian Filippo Villani, writing at the end of the fourteenth century, included him unhesitatingly among the *uomini illustri* of his city, and Petrarch in his will made the precious bequest to Francesco Carrara, Lord of Padua, of a Madonna – 'a work by the eminent painter Giotto. ... The ignorant do not understand the beauty of this panel but the masters of art are stunned by it.'[3]

Giotto's glory remained intact during the following century. Ghiberti, the designer of the famous bronze doors of the Baptistery in Florence, and Leonardo da Vinci celebrated his memory. And in 1490, in order to give him a fitting memorial, Lorenzo Il Magnifico commissioned from Benedetto da Maiano a bust of Giotto in full relief for the cathedral. The humanist Angelo Poliziano composed the epitaph:

'I am he through whom painting, being dead, came once
    more to life,
He whose hand, so nimble and so delicate,
Could paint better than any other's.
What my art lacked was lacking from our very nature.
Do you admire a tower resounding with bells?
It rose to the stars by my craft.
In fine I am Giotto. What need to say more?
That name alone will do service for an ode.'[4]

And the praise lavished on Giotto by the Renaissance was to be echoed by later centuries. The numerous anecdotes about the painter that circulated among his contemporaries and were recorded by the storytellers throw some light on his personality. There was nothing 'artistic' in the modern sense about his temperament. He was neither a romantic nor a bohemian, neither a dreamer nor unbalanced; he was never in need of psychoanalysis. He was neither a visionary nor a martyr and he did not opt out of society – as Gauguin did.

Giotto was above all level-headed and balanced; a self-possessed realist untroubled by *Angst* or moral doubt; a man of action who preferred life to meditation. In many ways he anticipated rationalism; he was on the side of reason against emotion. He was, in fact, the first bourgeois painter.

Like many of the bourgeois of his period, Giotto knew how to profit from currency fluctuations. The income he drew from his industrially organized workshop he invested in real estate. His reputation as a wealthy landowner is well-established: Boccaccio speaks of his 'domain' and his 'estates' in the Mugello valley outside Florence. There are numerous contracts made before notaries which provide eloquent evidence of the fact that the painter devoted a considerable amount of his energies to making his capital bear fruit. He was for ever buying, selling, and leasing his farms, and was able to give his daughters handsome dowries.

On 14 January 1322 he bought several pieces of land:
Pace, son-of the late Bettino de Colle, of the Parish of S. Cassian of Padula, has, in his own right, sold, given, transferred and ceded to Giotto, son of the late Bondone, of the Parish of Santa Maria Novella, purchasing and receiving on his own behalf and on that of his heirs. ... First, sole metayage of a piece of land situated at Posatoia, in the Parish of S. Michele de Allioni. ... Item another piece of land situated at Posatoia. Item another piece of land situated in a place called Quercia *sole*, with two oaks at Colle. ...[5]

Another contract tells us that Giotto leased on a metayer basis a 'piece of land with house, yard, garden, vineyard, enclosure and arable land ... for one year in return for half the produce'.[6]

Sometimes there was litigation with neighbours, for instance with Ser Grimaldus about a 'piece of land situated at Camporitondo, Parish of S. Michele de Aglone, which the said Giotto claimed to be his. ...'[7] The marriage contract of Chiara, one of Giotto's daughters, with Zuccerino lists all the lands the painter gave her as dowry. Could it be that he married her for her dowry? If his contemporaries are to be believed, Giotto's family were well-known for their ugliness. In his commentary on *The Divine Comedy*, Benvenuto da

Imola tells how Dante encountered Giotto when he was at work on the Arena Chapel in Padua and fell into ecstasies over the paintings. Just then one of Giotto's sons arrived, and he was very ugly. Astonished by the young man's ugliness, Dante could not help exclaiming to the painter: 'How is it that you make painted figures so well and real ones so badly?' 'Because I do the former by day and the latter by night.' Giotto was celebrated for his wit.

Land was not Giotto's only source of profit. Other documents show that he engaged in strictly financial operations as well. He stood surety for a loan, and seems himself to have been something of a professional money-lender. In 1314 he hired six lawyers to prosecute the unfortunate debtors who could not pay up on time. Any kind of business was fair game to him. He shamefully exploited the weavers working in the country around Florence by renting looms to them at extortionate rates (120 per cent).[8]

On 4 September 1312: 'Giotto, painter, of the Parish of S. Maria Novella, has rented on his own behalf and on behalf of his heirs, to Bartolo Rinuccij, of the Parish of S. Trinita, for the six months following, a loom of foreign make, assessed by mutual agreement at 10 pounds of small florins, for a monthly rent of 20 soldi of small florins.'[9]

Giotto's own dynamic exuberance reflected the dynamism of the high bourgeoisie of Florence, who were to find in him the man suited to serve their interests. The years when Giotto was active coincided with the heyday of Florentine financial activity. He was twenty-six when the high bourgeoisie finally took over power in 1293, and he died in 1336, on the eve of a series of great bankruptcies that were to put an end to the financial hegemony of the city.

The year 1293 is important because it marks the retreat of the Florentine nobility from power and the advent of a society based on money and led by bankers. From this point of view it can be said to be a date in the history of capitalism. The Florentine bankers who employed Giotto were the bankers of Europe. They had branches in every country, and even financed kings. Princes relied on their reputation for financial

acumen, and constantly entrusted them with the administration of revenue and the management of loans.

The Florentines also financed the papacy. At the Jubilee of
1300 Boniface VIII, receiving embassies from the four corners
of Christendom, exclaimed as that of Florence came forward:

What a city, this Florence! Those who feed us, who
administer our court, are they not Florentines? They
seem to rule the entire world, for the ambassadors that
kings, barons and communes have been sending us have
all been Florentines. They must be the fifth element of
the universe.[10]

This striking public tribute to the Florentines bears witness to
the fact that the Church was now inextricably involved in the
bourgeois world of money. In the early fourteenth century the
Church could not, without condemning itself, adopt the ideas
of St Francis of Assisi who, a hundred years earlier, had
preached absolute poverty, declaring any possessions, however small, to be an obstacle to happiness and brotherhood. In
the quarrel within the Franciscan order between the
'spirituals', faithful to the spirit of poverty of the founder, and
the 'conventuals', who stood for a compromise between poverty and property, the papacy could not but side with the
latter.

Through the General of the Franciscans, Giovanni da
Muro, the Roman Curia commissioned Giotto to paint the
life of St Francis in the basilica at Assisi, fully confident that he
would fulfil his commission in the spirit of the conventuals.
Giotto brought his own particular genius to the task. Giotto is
revered by millions of people all over the world as the faithful
painter of the Poor Man of Assisi. In fact St Francis must have
turned in his grave to be traduced by Giotto, the hated
representative of that very world of money which he had
fought against until there was no strength left in his body.
St Francis would have torn down the frescoes and had the
basilica destroyed.

Faithful to the directives he doubtless received from Rome,
Giotto represented the saint as acting in full accord with the
papacy. He is shown not among the poor but in high bour-

geois circles, and appears in robust health, whereas we know that the hardships he imposed upon himself made him emaciated and ill. Even the background is travestied: the little church of S. Damiano, which Giotto knew well, appears covered with a luxurious marble façade.

We know how Giotto felt about poverty from a *canzone* he composed on the subject. He was not enthusiastic. For him involuntary poverty 'which comes to us in spite of ourselves, is all sorrow – there can be no doubt of this: it leads to sin, it often deprives women and girls of their honour and makes men commit theft, violence and villainy.'

As for voluntary poverty, it is nothing but hypocrisy:

We see often with our own eyes that the man who praises poverty has no peace, and seeks all the time to throw it off. Should some honour or great appointment come his way, he pounces on it like a hungry wolf. He knows how to obtain his purpose by hiding it and covers himself so well that, though the most wicked wolf, he appears, under his false cloak, the most innocent lamb. By such devices does this 'spoilworld' thrive, so long as this hypocrisy is not destroyed which leaves no part of the world untouched by its art. Go, my song, and if you encounter proud men (or charlatans), reason with them in order to convert them. If they resist be bold enough to drown them.[11]

The Florentine Commune, led by the principal bourgeois families, could hardly have found an artist more devoted to its cause than Giotto, author of a poem against poverty, businessman and usurer. For the great hall of the Palazzo del Podesta he was commissioned to paint a vast allegory on a topical theme: the Commune Despoiled – despoiled, of course, by the other social classes.

Painting at that time was used as a psychological and political weapon. Those who offended against the bourgeois order, traded dishonestly, or went bankrupt were shown in humiliating postures, with a rope round their necks, on the walls of the Palazzo del Podesta or on the city gates. In the last decade of the thirteenth century a defamatory painting was put up of a nobleman who had robbed a merchant crossing the territory of the Republic of Florence.

It was out of political opportunism that the Bardi, bankers to the Roman Curia, commissioned Giotto to paint the life of St Francis, a theme dear to the papacy, in their chapel at Santa Croce. Frescoes like this carried prestige value, and can be compared with the large private collections of this century. The Peruzzi, the Guigni, and the Toringhi-Spinelli families who made Florence the most powerful city in Europe, also had chapels in Santa Croce and commissioned Giotto to decorate them.

So that he might inherit the estate of his father, Enrico Scrovegni – the richest man in Padua, who had been excommunicated for usury – was obliged, for part of his penance, to build a church. It is known as the Arena Chapel. Scrovegni invited Giotto help him 'clear' his family. Giotto responded and set about what was to be one of his most remarkable masterpieces.

In the main scene on the back wall, instead of showing Enrico offering the chapel to the Virgin in all humility in expiation of the sins of his family, Giotto made the revolutionary and almost blasphemous decision to paint Enrico the same size as the Virgin – in defiance of the tradition according to which the Mother of God must always be shown larger than an ordinary mortal. Not only did Giotto 'clear' the Scrovegni, he glorified them. And he put his heart into it: he was vindicating a fellow-usurer who had had the misfortune to be caught and excommunicated.

The painters of the period played a part in political life, at times a very active one. A few years before Giotto was appointed court painter to Robert of Naples, this king, whose claim to the throne was being challenged, put pressure on John XXII to have his brother Louis de Toulouse canonized. In 1317, having obtained satisfaction, he summoned Simone Martini in all haste and commissioned a picture of himself being crowned by his sainted brother. Thus Heaven gave its blessing to the usurper for all the world to see. This painting, which for art historians has presented primarily problems of style and form, had a precise political meaning for Martini's contemporaries. What Robert of Naples had commissioned was a piece of propagandist art.

The Church did the same thing. Painting was an instrument of policy. In the struggle for political supremacy between the papacy and the Holy Roman Empire a defender of the latter, Alexander of Roes, developed the idea that *both* institutions were needed for the moral government of humanity: 'Just as the Roman eagle cannot fly with only one wing, so the bark of Peter cannot be kept to its course through the storms and swells of this world by one oar alone.'[12]

To answer this challenge to his power and to impress on the minds of all the determination of the papacy to fulfil its mission of governing the world alone, Boniface VIII commissioned Giotto in 1298 to make a vast mosaic at St Peter's in Rome of the scene on the sea of Galilee. The bark of the Apostles is caught in the storm, it is guided by Christ, and rowed by St Peter – with a single oar. The mosaic made a great impression on the faithful. When Catherine of Siena saw it – the Popes were at the time in exile in Avignon – the thought that 'she alone' would have to hold the heavy oar of the bark of the Church produced spasms in her body which became a permanent affliction.

In the Middle Ages fixed images had the same evocative power that film and television have today. Until Giotto, painting lagged behind sculpture in this respect. What Giotto's contemporaries admired most, and what undoubtedly contributed most to his fame, was the 'photographic realism' of his renderings. The witnesses all agree: it is like looking at reality itself. This pursuit of 'photographic reality' was to become one of the main ambitions of the painters of our civilization until the day when, in 1839, Daguerre commercialized photography. From then on painting had to take a different direction. The Impressionists and Cézanne understood this and developed non-photographic painting which led through cubism to abstraction and the dissolution of form.

The chronicler Giovanni Villani says that Giotto was 'the

one who came closest to the natural in the rendering of figures and actions'.[13] And Boccaccio writes:

Giotto had so excellent a mind that there was nothing in nature, mother of all things operating by the continuous movement of the heavens, that he could not depict with stylus and pen or with the brush so accurately that it seemed not a copy but the very thing itself, so much so that in front of his work men's senses were often deceived, believing what was painted to be true.[14]

This text reveals the admiration of the fourteenth-century spectator for Giotto's discoveries in perspective. He painted false cornices that seemed real. He was the first painter to make a rigorous application of geometrical perspective, based on the convergence of lines towards a vanishing point. In this field he anticipated the great painters of the following century: Uccello, Piero della Francesca, and Mantegna.

Giotto also painted portraits that were praised as excellent likenesses. Filippo Villani, nephew of Giovanni, says that Giotto's images 'agree so well with the traits of nature that they seem to be alive and breathe; and his likenesses render actions and gestures so appropriately that they seem to speak, weep, rejoice and do other things not without delighting the spectator who praises the artist's mind and hand'.[15]

In Padua Giotto painted Enrico Scrovengni, and in Florence portraits of the Peruzzi. In Rome Boniface VIII, who had a taste for portraits and used to send his own to conquered cities as a sign of authority, commissioned Giotto to paint him blessing the crowd. This desire for self-representation made his enemies accuse him of idolatry. Dante, who put Boniface in Hell, includes him, no doubt, in the taunt against corrupt popes who differ from the idolater only in that he worships one, whereas they worship a hundred.[16]

The portrait of Dante in the chapel of the Palazzo del Podesta in Florence is a posthumous one. The poet who sided with the Empire in its struggle against the papacy would no doubt have refused to sit for the painter who worked all his life for the Roman theocracy and its allies. He cannot have approved of any of Giotto's works: the 'Navicella' (the bark of the Apostles), the portrait of Boniface VIII (whom Dante also accused of simony), or the Assisi frescoes. Dante himself always insisted on the fundamental importance of the ideal of poverty.

How can this political disagreement be reconciled with those three lines of Dante which would seem to be a paean of praise for the painter?

> Cimabue thought he held the field
> In painting, and now the cry is for Giotto,
> So that the other's fame is now obscured.

Few historians have taken the trouble to study the context. The lines come from Canto XI of *Purgatory*, which is devoted to the proud. Dante is not in the least concerned to celebrate the renown of the painters he mentions but only to remark how brief it is and how subject to fashion. He goes on:

> Earthly fame is nothing but a breath of wind,
> Which first blows one way and then blows another,
> And brings a fresh name from each fresh direction.[17]

And he denounced worldly success of this kind as a form of arrogance and pride.

Painter and poet also differed in their birth: the one came from humble origins, the other from an old Florentine family. Differences in education were a further obstacle to their mutual understanding. Giotto's education was perfunctory; he doubtless had the same schooling as other painters and manual workers, that is, the primary education of the Mechanical Arts. Dante had a university education in the Liberal Arts.

In his writings Dante shows the academic intellectual's contempt for manual workers and for those without higher education. Western academics of our own day often display the same contempt for people who do not belong to their caste.

But in spite of Dante, Giotto's fame continued to grow after the poet's death in 1321. In 1330 Giotto became a member of the household of the King of Naples and in 1334 he was given a major appointment in Florence. He died on 8 January 1336 and was 'buried by the Commune in Santa Reparata [i.e. the Cathedral] with great honour'.

Soon after his death European capitalism experienced its first crisis. The London branches of the Bardi and the Peruzzi (Giotto's patrons at Santa Croce) went bankrupt in 1339, when the King of England repudiated his debts amounting to 1,365,000 florins. The head offices followed suit in 1343 and 1346. The memory of these bankruptcies has remained so vivid in Italy that during the Second World War Mussolini is said to have demanded that England repay the debt – with interest. These bankruptcies plunged Florence into an economic crisis without precedent. The high bourgeoisie was now forced to share power with the middle and lower ranks of the bourgeoisie, and for a time, following the revolt of the Ciompi in 1378, even with the proletariat. It did not regain sole power until 1393.

Most art historians deplore the fact that during this period Giotto's successors failed to develop or even maintain his discoveries and innovations. They point out that no painter dared to represent a donor the same size as holy personages. These facts reflect the brake put on rationalism and the self-confidence of the bourgeoisie by the economic crisis.

Had Giotto lived longer he, too, would have ceased to paint like Giotto.

3 □ Towards the Liberal Arts

In his celebrated treatise on painting, compiled in Florence during the first third of the fifteenth century, Cennino Cennini testifies to the ascendancy of Giotto over his successors, though, of course, he has no conception of the social and psychological factors that helped this painter's personality to develop so fully: 'Giotto reconverted the profession of painting from Greek to Latin and made it modern. He possessed more perfect skill than anyone has possessed since.'[1]

Cennini introduces himself in these words:

I, Cennino, son of Andrea Cennini, of Colle di Valdessa, was trained in this profession for twelve years by my master, Agnolo di Taddeo, of Florence. He learned it from Taddeo, his father, who had been christened by Giotto and had been his pupil for twenty-four years. ... To help those who wish to enter this profession, I will set down what the said Agnolo taught me and what I have tried out and verified with my own hand.[2]

Cennini's handbook is interesting for what it tells us about the standard of instruction and the kind of knowledge current among the painters of the period; we gain some idea of the intellectual gulf that must have separated a Giotto from a Dante. The tone of the work is similar to that of another book, written three centuries before and attributed to the monk Theophilus. Both begin with the history of the creation of the world.

Cennini describes in detail how to make colours, glues, brushes – miniver and hog's bristle – and how to prepare wall surfaces for fresco. He then explains how to paint in oils, how to distribute light and shade, how to differentiate, in terms of flesh tints, between the face of a youth and the face of an old man. This technical knowledge was handed on in the workshops from one generation to the next.

Chapter LXX of Cennini's handbook (there are 189 altogether) deals with the proportions of the human body, more precisely of the male body, for of the female body, writes Cennini, 'I will not speak, for it has no perfect proportion.' 'A man is as tall as the extended span of his arms. The arms, including the hands, reach to the middle of the thigh. The height of a man is eight times that of his face. A man has one rib less than a woman, on the left side.'[3]

These proportions (obviously wrong) are the same as those given by Giotto. The painters who followed him never bothered to verify his specifications. In fairness to them it must be said that the historical period following the death of Giotto and the temporary eclipse of the rationalism of the high bourgeoisie did not favour the spirit of inquiry. And the assertion that a man has one rib less than a woman suggests that autopsy was not yet practised by painters.

Cennini's handbook is concerned entirely with the technique of painting; there are no theoretical or scientific observations, no reference to problems of optics or perspective. Mathematics is absent from his manual. None of this is surprising; it is typically the work of a man brought up within the framework of the Mechanical Arts.

Cennini's education, like Giotto's, was that received by all manual workers, whether they were stone-cutters, smiths, potters, or weavers. Education in the Mechanical Arts was altogether different from the system of the Liberal Arts, abstract and theoretical, taught at universities to the privileged classes of society who could afford the fees. The lower classes, the peasants, the workers, the small traders, whose financial resources were limited had only one possibility open to them: to apprentice their children from the age of ten onwards in workshops. Here, depending on the trade, they learned reading and writing in the vernacular and perhaps a few rudiments of geometry or practical arithmetic.

The course of instruction was regulated by the guilds. Cennini tells us that he remained in the service of one master for thirteen years:

Know that this is the time you need in order to learn. First you need a year to study the elementary drawing which you execute on panels. Then you need six years to stay with a master in his shop to gain a knowledge of all the branches of our art (profession) beginning by preparing pigments, boiling sizes and grinding gessos, to acquire practice in preparing altar panels, modelling them and scraping them, gilding and stamping. Then in order to practise colouring, embellishing with mordants, doing cloths of gold and to get used to working on walls, you need another six years, drawing all the time, never leaving off, neither on holidays nor on working days.[4]

The guilds not only regulated apprenticeships and manufacture but also controlled the movements of their workmen outside their own town walls, and prohibited the employment of strangers within their town. Painters and sculptors in particular were constantly hampered by these restrictions.

The distinction between the Mechanical Arts, which implied physical labour directed to the shaping or transformation of materials, and the Liberal Arts, which were highly intellectualized and concerned with thought and the manipulation of pure concepts, was an inheritance from antiquity.

In the Middle Ages and the Renaissance period the Liberal Arts were taught at Arts Faculties which conferred degrees of Bachelor and Master of Arts. These degrees gave access to the higher faculties of canon law and theology. The medieval 'Arts' consisted of the seven Liberal Arts, which were subdivided into two groups: the Trivium and the Quadrivium. The Trivium included grammar, rhetoric, and dialectic; the Quadrivium arithmetic, geometry, astronomy, and music. Thus of what we today call 'the arts' only music was included. And even in this case it was the science of music that was studied, hand in hand with the speculative sciences – music as the queen of the immaterial realm of sounds. St Augustine considered music as a mathematical science. His *De musica* is a treatise on rhythm. The medieval musician who 'knew' musical theory was regarded more highly than the singer or the instrumentalist who translated it into sounds.

The Quadrivium was dominated by mathematics, and when painters and sculptors later began to claim equality with the Liberal Arts they attempted to show that their art required the knowledge of theoretical mathematics.

Ghiberti was the first painter or sculptor to achieve some success in the struggle to achieve parity with the Liberal Arts. The times were favourable to this progress. Born in 1378, the year of the revolt of the Ciompis, Ghiberti was fifteen when the great bourgeois families of Florence regained their full power. They no longer feared either the nobility or the lower classes, but they were also no longer animated by the creative energies of a rising class. They produced sons who were indifferent or hostile to business and whose preoccupations were henceforth to be literary. These scholars or men of letters were in fact the first humanists of the Renaissance, men with a passionate interest in antiquity. Supported by their family wealth, they devoted themselves to study, acquired manuscripts of ancient Greek and Roman authors, translated them or had them translated, and thus assembled scholarly libraries. They also began to collect antique objects.

Ghiberti was to be the court sculptor of this bourgeoisie as Giotto had been the court painter of its forerunner in the first third of the fourteenth century. Like Giotto, Ghiberti knew how to manage his own affairs. His annual tax-returns show the distribution and the growth of his wealth. But there the parallel ends, for thanks to his contact with these bourgeois humanists, Ghiberti discovered an intellectual vocation of his own. His commissions introduced him to men like Leone Battista Alberti and Niccolo Niccoli who allowed him to use their libraries. There he became acquainted with ancient authors, in particular with Vitruvius and Pliny, who had a profound influence on him, as indeed they were to have on many other men of the Renaissance interested in the problems of the painter, the sculptor, and the architect in antiquity.

Vitruvius, a Roman architect contemporary with Augustus and a man of the Mechanical Arts, wrote a treatise on architecture in ten books (dedicated to the Emperor) which contains the sum of the architectural knowledge of the period. The work was aimed at the *litterati* as much as if not more than at architects, for Vitruvius wanted to prove that the architect was worthy of the Liberal Arts. In order to perform his task a real architect needed a liberal education:

> He must be able to express himself well, be skilful with the pencil, instructed in geometry, with a wide historical knowledge, a diligent disciple of the philosophers, understanding music, not ignorant of medicine, acquainted with the opinions of the jurists, informed about the stars and the laws of heavenly phenomena.[5]

In his attempt to raise the architect to the level of the Liberal Arts, Vitruvius next tries to demonstrate that the architect is a disinterested person, for one of the reproaches of the men of letters was that the men of the Mechanical Arts worked for money: 'I, on the other hand, Caesar, have not applied myself to making money out of my art but have opted for slender means and a good reputation rather than for abundance and disrepute.'[6]

Pliny the Elder, who died a victim of his thirst for knowledge (in AD 79, trying from too close quarters to watch the eruption of Vesuvius, which engulfed Herculaneum and Pompeii), wrote the *Natural History*, a work of encyclopaedic range and our principal literary source of information about painters and sculptors in antiquity. In it Pliny retails several anecdotes about painters refusing money for their work. Thus at the end of his life Zeuxis gave away his paintings on the ground that they were 'priceless'.

Another anecdote, which concerns Apelles daring to remark to Alexander, who was holding forth in his workshop, that 'the boys grinding the colours are laughing at you',[7] gives the impression that painters and sculptors were held in exceptional regard in ancient Greece and Rome. But this is not the case. They were manual workmen, men working for wages. Since they existed to serve the taste for luxury, they sinned against civic morals. Even if their work was appreciated, the men themselves were dissociated from this: 'We admire the work, but we despise the workmen,' as Seneca and Plutarch put it. Thus the anecdotes recorded about them are often unreliable. They have been embellished and spread by the painters themselves in their desire to raise the prestige of their craft. The archives, such as the building accounts of the Erechtheum for the years 409–407, tell their own story. The painters employed were paid by the piece or by footage, and nothing distinguished them from the workmen who erected the scaffolding:

> To a painter, for painting 14 coffer-lids upon the ceiling, upon the beams above the image ... @ 4 drachma for each coffer-lid.
> To painters in encaustic, for painting the cymatium on the inner epistyle ... @ 5 obols a foot.
> For putting up a scaffolding for the painters in encaustic, in the interior, beneath the ceiling, to Manis, living in Kollytos ... 1 drachma 3 obols.[8]

Sculptors for their part were paid at the uniform rate of 60 drachma for a man or a horse.

In order to reinforce his claim that painting was held in great esteem in ancient Greece, Pliny had recourse to his vivid imagination. 'Ever since, it has never ceased to be held in high esteem, for not only men of good family but also men of high rank have engaged in it, and it is forbidden to slaves. Hence no work of painting or engraving has been fashioned by a slave's hands.'[9]

These assertions are flatly contradicted by an analysis of the building accounts for the Erechtheum. Marie Delcourt, who has studied these accounts, writes in her *Périclès*:

> Out of the seventy-one contractors and workmen whose political status we know, twenty were Athenians, not even a third; of these not one was a stonemason, a profession considered too rough and exhausting ... the goldsmith and the painter were foreigners ('*metics*') or slaves, so were nine out of ten decorators and five sculptors out of eight.[10]

Pliny's distortions of the truth were to have a marked influence on the humanists' attitude to painters and sculptors, and the latter were to find in the *Natural History* a justification for their social and intellectual ambition.

The study of Vitruvius and Pliny not only convinced Ghiberti that he must raise sculptors and painters from the Mechanical to the Liberal Arts but also suggested how he should set about it: by demonstrating that a sculptor could also be a scholar and a man of letters. In 1447 he published his *Commentarii*, borrowing the title from humanist writings. The work is fundamentally different from that of Cennini and has nothing in common with a traditional treatise on the Mechanical Arts. There are no descriptions of craft processes, for this is not a technical study – it is a work with scientific aspirations.

The *Commentarii* consists of three books. In the first Ghiberti recounts after Pliny the lives of the ancient painters and sculptors, offering them as examples to inspire his contemporaries. In the second he reviews the history of painting and sculpture in Italy up to his own time, discussing the merits of individual works and recognizing the crucial role of Giotto; he also writes about himself, his life and his works.

This is an event – the first autobiography of a sculptor. Ghiberti tells us in detail about the competition organized by the Arte di Calimala for the baptistery door of the cathedral of Florence, and his victory over Brunelleschi, who was later to have the glory of building the famous dome:

> There were six of us in the contest which was in great part a demonstration of the art of sculpture. The palm of victory was awarded to me – by all the experts and all those who competed with me. The honour was conceded to me universally and without exception. I appeared to everybody to have surpassed the others at that time without exception, the matter having been carefully considered and scrutinized by learned men.[11]

And when Ghiberti says with some vanity that 'few important works executed in our territory were not designed or supervised by me',[12] the voice is almost that of a twentieth-century painter or sculptor.

The third book expounds the scientific knowledge that a painter, a sculptor, or an architect should possess. It contains a discussion of optics and perspective for which Ghiberti drew on Avicenna, Alhazen, Witelo, and Roger Bacon; and a discussion of anatomy based on Averroes. Ghiberti has not always fully assimilated the works he has read, but we are a long way from Cennini with his notion that a man has one rib less than a woman. Ghiberti discusses the proportions of the human body according to Vitruvius and as propounded by Giotto. The proportions are more accurate. Basing himself again on Vitruvius he recommends the study of arithmetic, history, medicine, and philosophy – in fact an encyclopaedic education conceived in the spirit of the Liberal Arts.

In their ascent towards the status of the Liberal Arts, painters, sculptors, and architects found their cause taken up by a humanist who had also read Pliny. His intervention was decisive. When a man of letters, educated in the Liberal Arts, became the personal friend of these men of the Mechanical Arts – Brunelleschi, Donatello, Luca della Robbia, and Ghiberti – this was an important event. What is more, this humanist himself was a painter and an architect. This early ally was Leone Battista Alberti. Descended from a long line of Florentine nobles, he completed his studies in Bologna, where he studied canon law. He became known in literary circles by some of his writings and is famous for deceiving the humanists with a play he wrote himself, *Philodoxeus*, which specialists attributed to Lepidus, a Latin author. He subsequently wrote a monumental treatise on architecture in ten books, modelled on Vitruvius.

In 1435 Alberti published in Florence a Latin treatise on painting, and the following year a translation in the vernacular so that painters could read it. The work caused a sensation and a scandal in humanist circles. To write a theoretical work on painting and sculpture was to place these on the same intellectual level as the Liberal Arts. What a thing for a man of letters to suggest! To justify this heresy, this intellectual treason, Alberti stresses first of all the role of geometry, one of the seven Liberal Arts, in painting:

I would wish the painter to be as learned as he can in all the Liberal Arts but first of all I want him to know geometry. I agree with the saying of Pamphilus, the ancient and most excellent painter from whom young nobles began to learn to paint. He held that no painter could paint well if he did not know much geometry.[13]

Alberti then deals at length with geometry and linear perspective: 'And we shall be content if this certainly difficult subject and one that has not to my knowledge been treated before will in one way or another be understood by him who reads us.'[14]

Alberti was right, the subject was difficult for the level of instruction of painters at the time. It took about twenty years before painters succeeded in applying in their work the rules of perspective set out in the treatise.

To convince the humanists that painters and sculptors deserve to be treated with respect and on a footing of equality, Alberti piles up evidence of the esteem in which they were held in antiquity. One might think, to read him, that all the great men of the past had been painters. He would have his reader know that the nobles in antiquity did not consider painting a dishonourable activity. His source is obviously Pliny and he follows closely a passage we have already quoted when he writes: 'Painting was held in such esteem and honour among the Greeks that they made an edict and a law prohibiting slaves from learning to paint.'[15]

But as we have already seen, the authenticity of this edict must be taken with a pinch of salt. Like Pliny, Alberti allows his imagination free range and ends by convincing himself that painting is one of the disciplines of the Liberal Arts (which Pliny himself had not dared to assert!): 'Acmilius Paullus, and not a few other Roman citizens, as part of the good [i.e. liberal] arts ... taught their sons painting.'[16] The passage on which this is based says merely that, in response to Acmilius Paullus' request for a philosopher to educate his children and a painter to decorate his triumph, the Athenians sent Metrodorus who was both.

The significance we have attributed to the existence of the two courses of education, the mechanical and the liberal, is

pointed up in a dramatic way in the notebooks of Leonardo
da Vinci. A great deal has been written about Leonardo.
Freud has even psychoanalysed some of his works. But what
no one has revealed, and what he suffered from most, is the
humanists' contempt for him. They considered him a man of
the Mechanical Arts, which he was. He never had the opportunity to go through the course of the Liberal Arts. He had
little Latin and no Greek. Time and again in his writings he
returns to this scorn of the academics:

> Because I am not a literary man [*litterato*] some pre-
> sumptuous persons will think that they may reasonably
> blame me by alleging that I am an unlettered man [*homo
> sansa lettere*]. Foolish men! ... They will say that because
> I have no letters [*per non avere io littere*] I cannot express
> well what I want to treat of.[17]

He questions the right of these *litterati* to judge him:

> They go about puffed up and pompous, dressed and
> decorated with the fruits not of their own labours but
> those of others. And they will not allow me my own. And
> if they despise me an inventor, how much more could
> they – who are not inventors but trumpeters and de-
> claimers of the works of others – be blamed.[18]

He reproaches writers with having excluded painting from the
Liberal Arts: 'it is wrong, writers, to have left her out of the
number of the Liberal Arts'.[19] If music is a liberal art, then
how much more so painting: 'Since you have put music
among the Liberal Arts, you must either put painting there as
well, or else withdraw music.'[20] If painting is a mechanical art
because it is manual, then so is writing: 'If you call painting
mechanical because it is at first manual, because the hands
represent what they find in the imagination, you writers draw
with the pen manually that which is found in your minds.'[21]

Leonardo's anger against the humanists shows also that they
associated the Mechanical Arts with 'filthy lucre': 'And if you say
painting is mechanical because it is done for a price, who falls
into this error, if error it can be called, more than you? ... If you
lecture in class rooms, do you not go where you are best paid? ...
Do you do any work without some payment?'[22]

Nevertheless if Leonardo fought with energy to introduce painting into the sanctuary of the Liberal Arts, he considered sculpture unworthy of the honour. This was aimed at his rival, Michelangelo. He thus launched a quarrel which was to have a long and passionate sequel.

> Sculpture is not a science but a most mechanical art because it brings sweat and bodily fatigue to him who works at it. ... The sweat combines with dust and becomes mud with the face caked and the rest covered all over with marble dust so that he [i.e. the sculptor] looks like a baker, and covered with minute chips so that he looks as if it had snowed on him, and his house is dirty and full of chips and stone dust.[23]

The painter, on the contrary,

> sits at great ease in front of his work, well-dressed, and moves his very light brush dipped in pleasing colours. He is dressed as well as he likes and his house is full of fine pictures and clean, and there is often musical accompaniment or reading aloud of various beautiful books which, not being mixed with the striking of hammers or other noises, is heard with great pleasure.[24]

Under the assaults of men like Ghiberti, Alberti, and Leonardo, the stronghold of the Liberal Arts began to crack before the end of the century. By a literary *coup d'état* the Neoplatonist humanist, Marsiglio Ficino (1433–99), upset the hierarchy of the Arts. He unofficially placed painting, sculpture, and architecture among the Liberal Arts. Of the traditional ones he kept grammar, rhetoric, and music; he replaced dialectic with poetry, he also introduced the ancient songs sung to the Orphic lyre, and ruled out with a stroke of the pen arithmetic, geometry, and astronomy. 'For this century has brought back to light the liberal disciplines which had become nearly extinct, grammar, poetry, oratory, painting, sculpture, architecture, music, the ancient chant of songs to the Orphic lyre. And this in Florence.'[25]

Ficino's *coup d'état* introduced such confusion into the terminology of the Arts, which today are called Fine Arts, that even dictionaries offer conflicting information about their number and relative importance. The Dictionary of the French Academy under *Art* has the following entry: 'Fine Arts or simply the Arts *par excellence*. Painting, sculpture, architecture, engraving, music and dance ... to these are sometimes joined eloquence and poetry.'

Littré's dictionary, on the other hand, does not consider engraving to be an art, makes no reservations about eloquence and poetry, and thinks that dance is an art only in a subsidiary sense: '*The Fine Arts*: music, painting, sculpture, architecture, eloquence and poetry, and in a subsidiary way, dance.'

In this confusion one thing is certain – the arts once known as Mechanical, and spurned as such, now occupy the place of honour.

4 □ The Artist is born

The metamorphosis of painters and sculptors from plain mortals into artists, beings endowed with divine powers, is the work of the Neoplatonist humanists patronized by the Medici.

From the second third of the fifteenth century onwards the history of Florence is that of the Medici. The great Florentine families which had made the Republic powerful handed the reins of government to this one family, which began to move towards monarchical rule. The Medici were patrons of art, the most famous in history; but, like most other patrons, they patronized at the expense of the man in the street.

Cosimo de' Medici initiated this evolution towards personal rule in 1434. He did not suppress republican institutions, he simply weakened and circumvented them. Elections to public offices continued to be held but became a formality. Cosimo, the richest banker in Europe, made use of his wealth but took care not to parade it. He influenced public opinion through the writers he protected. To Marsiglio Ficino and the other humanists who revived Plato – Landino, Poliziano, Pico della Mirandola – he presented villas in Careggi and Fiesole. In return they dedicated their works to him. Quietly Cosimo deprived Florence of her liberties.

This evolution towards personal rule gathered speed under his grandson, the most famous of the Medici, Lorenzo Il Magnifico. Lorenzo had been brought up as a gentleman, a poet, a friend of the humanists and a humanist himself. The appearances of republicanism which Cosimo had kept up now began to fade away. Lorenzo established relations with the sovereigns of all Europe on a footing of equality. His lavish entertaining, the succession of feasts he organized and his intensive patronage of art soon brought him to the brink of bankruptcy. Unfortunately for Florence, the prince had taken over from the banker.

To escape bankruptcy, Lorenzo

> to whom his bank's finances and those of the State were all one, speculated with public funds, suspended the payment of dividends out of the public debt ... increased taxes, abolished charitable foundations, underpaid his mercenary troops. All this was not enough and finally the city itself had to go bankrupt in order to save the Medici bank from failure. An official commission of seventeen members reduced the interest on the public debt from 5 to 3 per cent and from 3 to 1½ per cent ... it debased the coinage in such a way that the taxpayers paid in good money and the State in bad. Lorenzo was saved but Florentine credit suffered a blow from which the city never entirely recovered.[1]

The great patrons, donors, and builders, like Lorenzo Il Magnifico, who are celebrated out of all proportion, should rather be condemned by humanity, for their activities caused inflation and misery. It matters not whether they be called Pharaoh, King Solomon, Emperor Justinian, Duc de Berry, Leo X, Shah Djahan, or Louis XIV. To this list can be added the 'robber barons', the American multimillionaire collectors. And many others!

If the Medici were partly responsible for the economic decline of Florence and the loss of its liberties, the humanists they patronized must also share this responsibility. They did not oppose the trend towards despotism. Theirs was a treason of the intellectuals. Immersed in the Graeco-Roman past which they rediscovered and set about reconstituting, they ignored the world evolving around them. They fled from reality and lived in closed circles to which only initiates were admitted. They lost touch with the people and became contemptuous of them. Lorenzo could proclaim his contempt for 'the little people' without protest from his friends: 'Only people of noble blood can truly conduct affairs to the point of perfection. There is no scrap of genius in the little people who work with their hands and have no time to cultivate their intelligence.'[2]

The chief luminary in this group of initiates, the one whose ideas were to have the greatest effect on posterity, was Marsiglio Ficino. He was the first head of what became known as the 'Academy of Careggi', in an allusion to Plato's Academy. They were said to keep an altar lamp burning in front of a bust of Plato. One of Ficino's leading ideas, and the one that had the greatest influence on the attitude of the *litterati* towards painters and sculptors, and on the new self-awareness of the painters and sculptors themselves, was the idea that man as the universal artificer who transforms the material inventory of the world – the elements, stones, metals, plants, animals – as though it were subject to him, resembles God.

Man creates like god. Ficino writes:

The (human) mind conceives in itself by thought all that God creates by thought in the world. It expresses this in audible speech, writes it with pen on paper, represents it in the matter of the world by what it makes. ... Man is god over all material elements, for he uses, modifies and forms them all.[3]

And he adds:

Since man has understood the order of the celestial spheres – from whence they are moved, where and in what measure they proceed, what they produce – who can deny that he is nearly of the same genius as the author of the spheres and that he could, in a certain sense, make the heavens if he could obtain the instruments and the celestial matter? Because now he is able to produce them, though of a different matter, but in a similar order.[4]

The idea of inspiration and of genius, a gift of God, was also formulated at Careggi.

It is writings like these that transformed painters and sculptors into divine beings. And so the 'Artist' was born. The other basic idea of Ficino's was that the spirit of the artist revealed itself entirely in his work:

All the works of the (human) artificer that relate either to sight or to hearing declare the entire mind of the artificer. Those that relate to the remaining three senses hardly anything. In pictures and in buildings the intention and the judgement of the artist shine forth. The disposition and, as it were, the figure of his soul can be seen in them. Thus the soul represents itself in these works, as the face of a man looking in a mirror represents itself in the mirror.[5]

This analogy of the mirror gave birth to the work of art. A work created by the artist was henceforth considered to be the reflection of an individual thought and no longer that of a superior idea. Form now tends to take precedence over content. The idea of intellectual property is born. And this interest in the work of art, which becomes a cult, gives birth, in turn, to a new religion – the religion of Art. The religion of form, of style, of beauty, of aesthetics (the word does not appear until the eighteenth century). Independent of the Church, this original religion was to remain confined to an intellectual élite. For the humanists, art became an integral part of the oral and intellectual life. One could dedicate one's life to art. Art was a refuge, a sacred precinct into which one withdrew to escape the sorrows and wickedness of the world.

The conquest of Gaul had less importance for the humanists than Caesar's *Commentaries*. The significance of the action gave way to the beauty of the style. An anecdote reflects this state of mind. A dying humanist refused a crucifix on the ground that it was ugly. The crucifix had become a work of art.

The work of art was now an end in itself and no longer a means of action. The movement of art for art's sake, which was to be developed in the nineteenth century, had already begun.

This cult still has many followers – too many followers – amongst the intelligentsia of contemporary Western Europe. The birth of the 'Artist' and the 'Work of Art' has had many consequences. The importance of the subject becomes blurred. What matters is to acquire a work from the hand of a particular master. People no longer wanted a 'Madonna' or a 'Descent from the Cross' but a Leonardo da Vinci, a Michelangelo or a Bellini. In 1501 Isabella d'Este, wishing to have a picture by Leonardo, left him free to choose the subject. She wrote to inquire whether 'he would undertake to paint a picture for our studio. If he consented we would leave the subject and the time to his choice.'[6] Michelangelo was asked for a painting or a sculpture at his discretion.

Such freedom was henceforward to be greatly valued by artists. In 1506 the humanist Bembo wrote of Giovanni Bellini that he 'prefers that very specific terms should not be laid down for him. It is his custom, as he says, always to let his mind wander freely over his paintings, which according to him can then satisfy the beholder.'[7]

This state of things foreshadows the 'motifs' of Manet and Cézanne, and hence non-figurative art and abstract art. There is a fundamental difference between the kind of commission given to Giotto and one given to Michelangelo, but works by Michelangelo and Nicolas de Staël differ only in degree.

Another consequence of the emergence of the work of art was the difficulty of evaluating it. How does one price a personality or an expression of feeling? Until then the value of a picture or piece of sculpture had been assessed according to a scale which took into account the time spent on it and the cost of the materials used. A new set of criteria had now be devised. In cases of disagreement experts were called in, men of taste. Other artists were consulted. Michelangelo arbitrated in a dispute of this kind by deciding that the buyer should pay 100 scudi per head painted.

The work of art soon became subject to the law of supply and demand. Marsiglio Ficino could hardly have foreseen that in giving birth to the work of art he had left the way wide open to the commercialization of painting and sculpture on a vast scale. And also to speculation. From the very beginning the religion of Art was also a religion of profit. The middle class lost no time in organizing the market in works of art, of which the principal beneficiaries were to be firstly the artists them-

selves and secondly the great ones of the world. The man in
the street was excluded from this traffic: he was neither rich
enough nor grand enough to be able to take part.

> [Andrea del Sarto] soon completed another picture
> for the King of France, at his request, being a lovely
> Madonna, which was immediately sent, the merchants
> receiving four times as much as they had paid for it.[8]

Leonardo's father, Ser Piero, could not, according to
Vasari, resist the temptation to make money out of his son's
reputation:

> Piero took Leonardo's work secretly to Florence and
> sold it to some merchants for 100 ducats, and in a short
> time it came into the hands of the Duke of Milan, who
> bought it of them for 300 ducats.[9]

This anecdote must not mislead us into pitying Leonardo's
lot; when he accepted the hospitality of Francis I he was given
a princely annual income.

Francis I in trying to acquire Italian works of art no doubt
caused a rise in prices, just as four centuries later American
multimillionaires were to do. And there was a great Florentine
merchant, Giovambattista della Palla, who knew how to
profit from this situation to satisfy the ambition of Francis I
just as in the twentieth century there was a great merchant,
Duveen, to satisfy that of the Americans.

Vasari complains that 'Giovambattista della Palla, having
bought as many notable sculptures and paintings as he could,
and having the rest copied, had thus despoiled Florence of a
quantity of choice things to furnish a suite of rooms for the
King of France, which was to be as rich as possible in such
decoration.' [10]

The law of supply and demand operated in favour of some
painters, like Raphael, who became rich and lived on a
princely scale with palaces and servants, and to the detriment
of others who lived in penury and led a bohemian style of life
anticipating the romantic artists of the nineteenth century.

Raphael was perfectly aware of the privilege enjoyed by
artists who were in fashion: 'I am paid for my work whatever
sum I deem fitting,' [11] he wrote to his uncle, Simone Ciarla.

Raphael grew rich in Rome from 1508 onwards by partici-pating, first as painter then as architect, in a piece of criminal *hubris*: the destruction of the old basilica of St Peter and the building of a new one, a monstrous monument to the personal ambition and megalomania of Julius II and Leo X. The latter was a Medici. Raphael received the money collected from indulgences granted to those who contributed towards the cost of the building. These indulgences were one of the causes of the Reformation and hence of the wars of religion. Like Bramante and Michelangelo, Raphael has blood on his hands.

As a papal groom of the chamber and Knight of the Spur, Raphael became a familiar figure in papal circles. He also became an intimate friend of Count Baldassare Castiglione, a humanist and author of a 'best-seller' of the time, *Il Cortigiano* (The Courtier). This was a manual of conduct for the perfect gentleman. Castiglione recommends courtiers to have an acquaintance with painting and sculpture in imitation of the ancients. This work was to have a considerable influ-ence on the attitude of the upper classes towards art and artists, comparable to that exercised by Alberti and Ficino on the humanists.

The new importance accorded to the artist and the work of art tended to reverse the traditional relationship between the painter and the commissioning or buying patron. It was no longer the artist who humbly sought protection from a great man but the pope or the emperor who was anxious to obtain a work by this or that painter or to sit for a portrait by him. The popes went to great lengths to secure the services of Michelangelo. When Charles V ennobled Titian by making him Count of the Sacred Palace of the Lateran, he acknow-ledged in the official document that this was to thank Titian for immortalizing him in his portraits.

And Aretino, the celebrated pamphleteer and blackmailer, had portraits executed by the most famous painters and sculptors of the day.

Raphael and Titian are the two painters who adapted themselves successfully to the new position of the artist in society. But there were many others who, as a result of the change, lost their psychological and social bearings. Vasari tells of artists feasting, amusing themselves, and generally living with little regard for those around them:

... who under pretext of behaving like philosophers, lived like swine, never washed their hands, face, head, or beard, did not clean their house, only made their beds once in two months, covered their table with drawing-sheets, and only drank from the flask or the bottle, a manner of living which they considered very fine.[12]

This bohemian existence described by Vasari, which fore-shadows that depicted by Murger three centuries later in his *Scènes de la vie bohème,* bears witness to the contempt of these artists for the settled and methodical life of the bour-geois. We have come a long way from Giotto, for whom the bourgeois life was an ideal. The artists of this period are described as bizarre, whimsical, eccentric, odd, capricious. They are subject to periods of depression and melancholy. They have acquired a reputation for being unreliable and unconventional. They despise the crowd and work for whom-ever they fancy and when they feel like it. Vasari says of Pontormo that: 'he would only work when he wished, and being often requested to do things by noblemen, and notably on one occasion by Ottaviano de' Medici, he would not serve them, but would then begin something for some plebian instead at a low price'.[13]

Many artists thus became unstable and ill-adapted to the society in which they had to live. The transmutation of paint-ers and sculptors into artists by Ficino's Neoplatonism was often a process which the men themselves found hard to assimilate.

The archetypal artist, the 'divine' Michelangelo, was him-self unstable, a child of Marsiglio Ficino, unable to adapt. The humanists' abstract ideas found their very incarnation in the sculptor. As an adolescent he absorbed Neoplatonic ideas in the circle of Lorenzo Il Magnifico, listening to the conversa-tions of Ficino, Landino, Pico della Mirandola, and Politian. Ficino's parallel between creation by God and creation by man made a profound impression on him. He, Michelangelo, is like God, for given the instruments and heavenly material he could fashion the heavens himself. And indeed does he not fashion the heavens, in a different matter, but according to the same principles?

Deified by his contemporaries – he was called 'divine' in his own lifetime – Michelangelo wanted to make sure posterity was left with an ideal image of himself. The halo of glory created by Vasari – 'that the world should marvel at the singular eminence of his life and works and all his actions, seeming rather divine than earthly'[14] – was not enough. Michelangelo suggested to one of his pupils, Condivi, that he should write the master's life. It is an extraordinary instance of auto-hagiography.

Imbued with his divinity, Michelangelo held his own against popes, the representatives of God on earth but not God themselves. He dared to provoke the public anger of Aretino, blackmailer and the first art critic, before whom trembled the three principal sovereigns of Europe (the Pope, Charles V, and Francis I), by refusing to favour him with a drawing. Aretino hit back with a pun – 'Michelangelo *di vino*'.

The Quattrocento humanists could hardly have imagined that in the following century a sculptor, one of those who had scarcely emerged from the inferior ranks of the Mechanical Arts, would eclipse the glory of literary men. This was a revolution in the history of ideas.

Another artist anxious to leave to posterity the image of an ideal being, in personal contact with God, was Benvenuto Cellini. In his memoirs, a fascinating cloak-and-dagger story, he attempts to justify his assassinations and confidently asserts that God has taken him into the secrets of His providence:

And there is something else that I do not wish to omit – the most astonishing thing that could happen to any man. I report it in order to prove that God deigned to choose me as one to whom the secrets of His providence should be entrusted. From the time when I saw these things [i.e. visions and premonitions] there remained

with me above my head a halo, a marvellous thing which
is visible to every sort of man I have chosen to show it to,
which have been very few.[15]

Michelangelo maintained a certain decorum in his relations
with the popes. Not so Cellini, who accused one of them of
acting like a wild beast and of believing neither in God nor in
the devil.

In this Cellini lacked gratitude, for by his own account the
popes often showed him esteem. Paul III, when reminded by a
courtier of Cellini's assassination of the Milanese Pompeo and
pressed on that account not to receive him replied: 'You do
not know the case as well as I do. You must understand that
men like Benvenuto, unique in their profession, ought not to
be bound by law; and he in particular, for I know how right he
is.'[16] The remark reflects the way artists thought of themselves
at the time. Men like Michelangelo and Cellini obviously
considered themselves to be unique. The laws and regulations
that simple mortals were expected to observe did not apply to
them.

Painters and sculptors had succeeded in their aim of breaking away from the traditional framework of the Mechanical
Arts and the guilds. But they were fated never to become
integrated into the system of the Liberal Arts. The artist was a
being society had not provided for.

It was Vasari, the enthusiastic biographer of these exceptional beings but also a painter himself, in the service of the
absolutist Cosimo de' Medici, the first Grand Duke of Tuscany, who devised an institutional framework worthy of the
new 'race' of artists, and in particular of his friend and idol,
Michelangelo. This was an academy inspired by the ideas of
Leonardo da Vinci and the literary and scientific academies
that had spring up in Italy. Leonardo conceived of an academy – the word appears in his writings – with a scientific and
theoretical syllabus of a university type basically different
from the 'applied' teaching of the Mechanical Arts. There was
to be instruction in the theory of perspective and proportion;
there was also to be drawing, both copying the drawings of
the masters and drawing from life.

Taking up these ideas, Vasari founded an embryonic university for artists, the first Academy of Art, in 1563. This was the culmination of the efforts of men like Ghiberti, Alberti, and Leonardo himself.

To free painters and sculptors from the bondage of the Mechanical Arts and establish them in the Liberal Arts, Cosimo de' Medici approved the statutes of the Academy on 13 January 1563, and accepted the title of protector. He appointed as president a connoisseur, V. Borghini, and as first director, Michelangelo. He nominated thirty-six painters and sculptors to be members. The painters and sculptors who were privileged to be selected thus escaped from the control of the guilds. Soon enrolment in these ceased to be obligatory, a recognition of the fact that as professional organizations they no longer suited the position of the artist in society. In the Academy teaching, the old master–apprentice relationship was replaced by a master–pupil relationship. Thanks to the Academy, the artist was now an intellectual and not a manual worker.

In founding the Academy, Vasari wanted to provide an institutional framework for the artist. He was successful. It was also his ambition to wean artists from a bohemian and unconventional way of life. Through the discipline imposed by the Academy, he was successful in this too. He supported his policy by his writings. In his lives of painters and sculptors he attempted to show that the bad name artists had already made for themselves in the sixteenth century was due to a lunatic fringe, and he dwelt on the achievement of painters such as Raphael, who led the exemplary life of a nobleman.

The Academy offered the artist social prestige and security. But in exchange for these it deprived him of his liberty. Vasari, the servant of the Medici, found the artist a niche in the hierarchy of a despotic regime. A century later the authoritarian regime of Colbert and Louis XIV was to find in Vasari's Academy a convenient model, and Lebrun was to take at Versailles the role Vasari had played in Florence. And by the same token, Vasari's Academy is also the ancestor of the modern Soviet Academy.

5 □ The Church versus the freedom of the artist

V asari's efforts to wean artists from their bohemian way of life and their non-conformism were reinforced in the very year he founded his Academy by the decision of the assembled Fathers of the Church at the Council of Trent, to take the artists in hand again. Subjects were to be prescribed for the defence of the Catholic Church and the propagation of the Faith and in order to combat the spread of the Reformation, which prohibited images in places of worship.

At its twenty-fifth and last session, held on 3–4 December 1563, the Council decreed:

> That no images should be exhibited in churches that are based on false doctrine and likely to be the occasion of dangerous error to the uneducated ... all impure display should be eliminated, all lasciviousness avoided so that images are not painted and adorned with wanton attractions. ... To ensure that this is faithfully observed, the Holy Council forbids anyone to exhibit, or to cause to exhibit in any place or church, even if in any way exempted [i.e. from ordinary hierarchical control], any unusual image unless the bishop has approved it.[1]

This decree of the Counter-Reformation limiting the freedom of the artist is a considerable and exceptional event in the history of Christendom. To find anything comparable one has to go back eight centuries, to the Second Council of Nicaea (AD 787) which ruled that:

> The making of pictures shall be determined not by the invention of painters but by the principles laid down by the Catholic Church and by tradition ... the conception [i.e. of a picture] and (the interpretation of) the tradition

are a matter for the fathers and not for the painter. Only
the skill required is the painter's. The ordinance of the
picture is also reserved for the holy fathers.[2]

This decree was a by-product of the Iconoclastic Controversy,
which agitated the Byzantine Empire in the eighth and ninth
centuries. The adherents of both the Reformation and the
Counter-Reformation referred frequently to this theological
dispute, the former siding with the iconoclasts (those hostile
to images) and the latter with the iconodules (or defenders of
images).

One of the most admirable sovereigns in history but also
one of the most frequently decried, Leo III, the Isaurian,
decided in 726 to have religious images covered and to forbid
their worship. The reasons for this decision were partly religious and partly military and economic. The images or icons
were often venerated in their own right by the people rather
than as representatives of divinity. To Leo this iconolatry was
a return to paganism not to be tolerated, and so he decided to
prohibit images. The military and economic reason for this
decision was the proliferation of monks who lived from the
sale of icons. According to a contemporary pamphlet the
world was divided into two equal parts – monks and laymen.
To resist the Arab invasions the Byzantine State needed men
and money. By depriving the monasteries of their principal
source of revenue, the sale of icons, Leo III reduced the
recruitment of monks to the benefit of the army and recovered
some of the monastic wealth which was exempt from taxes.

After a succession of bloody victories and defeats the iconoclastic emperors were finally vanquished during the course of
the ninth century. The iconodules then began to compile
manuals for painters laying down the choice of subject and
the manner of composition of religious images. These manuals, which remained in use in the Eastern Church after its
separation from Rome in the eleventh century (and are still in
use today), confined the freedom of inspiration and expression of painters and sculptors within strictly defined limits.

In the West, Charlemagne, who wanted to marry the
Byzantine Empress Irene, was drawn into the Iconoclastic

Controversy. He took up an intermediary position, substantially that of the Roman Church until the sixteenth century. In the *Libri Carolini*, written at his command by a court theologian, he condemned the impious adoration of images which very often came to be seen as pagan allegories, but forbade their destruction. They must be neither broken nor worshipped; they had an educational value for the masses.

Perhaps because the Roman Church was afraid of a return to the cult of images it never introduced manuals for painters and sculptors. On occasion, when it was necessary, the clergy could and did issue directives, but for the most part, and for several centuries, painters and sculptors remained free to follow their own inspiration in the choice of subject and manner of composition.

Alcuin, one of the later scholars summoned by Charlemagne, expresses the Western point of view on the problems of the image and the superiority of the written word over the image, of the writer over the sculptor and painter.

If you say [so the image-worshipper is apostrophized] that you preserve the purity of your faith in images ... then venerate counterfeit colours: we shall venerate, and gain access to, hidden meanings. Take delight in painted pictures: we shall take delight in the words of God. Attend to the figures of things in which there is neither sight nor hearing nor taste nor smell nor touch; we shall attend to the law of God which is perfect, in which is to be found the testimony of God's justice, His precepts, the fear of Him and His judgements. ... And if you, lover, or rather adorer, of images, murmur rancorously in your heart, saying: what need for all this digressing on rhetorical figures? understand that these are dearer to us than your painted images or pictures and that that is why we have digressed at such length. Understand that in the Scriptures and in scriptural figures we ... find delights and recreations you will not find at all in figures or pictures in which you claim to preserve the purity of your heart.[3]

And he adds: 'Unhappy the memory that, to remember

Christ who should never leave the heart of the just man, needs the visual aid of an image; that is incapable of having Christ present in itself unless ... it sees a painted image of him. For such a memory, nourished on images, does not come from the love of the heart but from the compulsion of sight.'[4]

The views expressed here were, in our opinion, shared by the majority of intellectuals throughout the Middle Ages and the Renaissance, until the Counter-Reformation and the birth of aesthetics. (And we should like to hope that they are shared in their heart of hearts by the intellectuals of our time.)

The history of Western Christendom is punctuated by outbursts of iconoclasm which in many ways foreshadow the Reformation. Is there not an obvious iconoclastic strain in the reaction of the Cistercian monks at the beginning of the twelfth century against the decadent luxury of the Order of Cluny? Painters and sculptors, those whom we call artists today, were banished from the monasteries of Cîteaux because the Order forbade not only all 'graven images' but also all colour. The walls of monastic churches were to remain bare.

St Bernard, the soul and inspiration of the Order, was eloquent in his denunciations of the sumptuous Cluniac churches: 'O vanity of vanities and yet more madness than vanity! The church glistens on all sides but the poor man is hungry. The walls of the church are covered in gold but her sons are naked.'[5] He found particularly offensive the paganism of some of the capitals which distracted the monks from their meditations:

And besides in the cloisters, in front of the reading brethren, to what purpose this ridiculous monstrousness, this marvellous misshapen shapeliness and shapely misshapeness? What for these unclean apes, savage lions, monstrous centaurs, half men, striped tigers, fighting knights, trumpeting huntsmen. ... It becomes pleasanter to read in the marbles than in the books and to spend all day marvelling at these singular creations rather than meditating on the law of God.[6]

Subjects like these were obviously not prescribed by

churchmen; no doubt the sculptors took them from popular traditions and legends often influenced by the East.

Like other reformers, St Bernard was concerned about the cost – which he judged unnecessary – of these images: 'For God's sake, if you are not ashamed of these stupidities why do you not at least regret the expense?'[7]

St Bernard's fulminations make one think already of the Reformation preachers denouncing the extravagance and paganism of Rome, but, in fact, his anger was confined within monastic walls. He agrees that the secular clergy may have to use images because its duty is both to the 'wise and the unwise'. To excite the devotion of the latter, the 'carnal folk', 'corporeal' ornaments are needed because spiritual ones would have no effect. St Bernard rejects images for his monks because their appeal is to the senses.

As the years passed this austerity weakened. Painters and sculptors were readmitted to the monasteries, and the Cistercian Order began to decline.

At the beginning of the thirteenth century another great reformer, St Francis of Assisi, banished from his Order all painting and nearly all architecture: 'A ditch, a hedge, nothing more; no wall in honour of St Poverty and St Humility; huts made of mud and wood; very small churches; and neither preaching nor any other consideration must lead the brethren to build large and richly ornamented temples.'[8] St Francis is said to have demolished with his own hands a building his brethren had erected in his absence and which he, no doubt, did not find sufficiently austere. This history of the Franciscan Order, the crises it went through, are marked by the quarrel we have already spoken about (p. 16) between the 'spirituals', faithful to the ideal of poverty, and the 'conventuals', who favoured a compromise.

In 1260, some thirty years after St Francis' death, a Chapter of the Order held at Narbonne promulgated constitutions which, while they reaffirm the dedication of the Order to austerity, show that breaches had already occurred. Similar enactments were made in Assisi in 1279 and in Paris in 1292. Paragraph 18 of Rubric 3 (On the observation of poverty) as promulgated by the Paris Chapter rules that:

No pictures of great value or fine workmanship shall be placed on the altar or elsewhere. And if stained glass or panels of this kind have been made they shall be removed by the Visitors. Transgressors of this constitution shall be severely punished and the heads of their houses irrevocably expelled, unless they are reinstated by the General.[9]

But when the building of the basilica of Assisi was planned, Elias, a Conventual Franciscan, did not hesitate to order a beating for Brother Leo, the beloved disciple of St Francis, whom the Saint used to call 'Little lamb of God'. For Brother Leo had dared to destroy the collection box for the building fund. Faced with such means of applying pressure the spirituals had to give way. St Francis was flouted. The artists made a triumphal entry into the basilica. And we have seen how in the fourteenth century Giotto, the representative of the world of money, betrayed the ideal of St Francis there. Once again painters and sculptors were associated with the decline of an Order.

Leo the Isaurian, St Bernard, and St Francis all manifested hostility to images, each in his own way; the same can be said of the Dominican monk Savonarola at the end of the fifteenth century. When one hears the passionate oratory of Savonarola's sermons preached in Florence, which dared to challenge and denounce not only the splendour of Lorenzo Il Magnifico's court and the paganism of his humanistic pursuits but also the depraved morals and the corruption of the Church of Rome, it is as if one were listening again to the words of his great predecessors: 'Take away from your room and from your house these improper paintings.' [10] 'Nowadays images in churches are made with such skill and are so ornate and elaborate that they destroy God's light and true contemplation, and what is considered is not God but only the skill that is in the images. ... There must be more simplicity.'[11] 'You who have your houses full of vanities and images.'[12]

To remedy this state of affairs, Savonarola appealed directly to the painters to make them aware of their responsibilities: 'You painters, you do wrong, if you knew the scandal that ensues and all that I knew, you would not want to paint. You introduce all the vanities into churches.'[13] Savonarola thought that artists could usefully serve the cause of God.

What was so extraordinary in this appeal was that it was heard. Many painters suddenly stopped painting nudes and pagan subjects: and at Savonarola's insistence they brought their works to be burned in public. Painters like Fra Bartolommeo became monks. Botticelli, who must have been the first painter to be engaged by the Neoplatonist humanists to express their ideas, stopped working for them.

Under the combined pressure of Pope Alexander VI, a Borgia not inclined to forgive his attacks on the corruption of Rome, and the Medici, to whose downfall he had contributed, Savonarola was arrested, tortured, and executed (1498). Florence went back to a life of pleasure, and for the time being Rome could abandon itself once more to the humanist artists, whose inspiration was untrammelled.

But a few years after the death of Savonarola, beyond the frontier of Italy, in Germany the voice of another monk, Luther, was raised like that of the Dominican, in denunciation of the unbridled extravagance and paganism of Rome. This time the danger for the Roman Church was much greater because Luther envisaged a popeless Christendom – Savonarola had merely wanted to reform the dissolute morals of the papacy. For the artist the danger was also greater because Luther only 'tolerated' images in his reformed church. 'I approached the task of destroying images by first tearing them out of the heart through God's word and making them worthless and despised. ... For when they are no longer in the heart, they can do no harm when seen with the eyes.'[14] Savonarola had at least granted their usefulness as a Bible for the illiterate.

Artists in Germany were soon confronted by a hard choice: Luther or Rome. For most Germans the problem was one of conscience but for the artist, whose means of livelihood was directly involved, it was to some extent a question of survival. If he opted for Luther he knew that he would no longer work for the Church, his chief patron so far. And some artists did sacrifice their standard of living to their conscience.

It can be said that up to 1527 artists in Italy were not affected either morally or materially by the reform movement north of the Alps. But in that year the Emperor's army, with Lutheran detachments in it, changed this situation by storming and sacking Rome and desecrating churches.

These dramatic events finally awakened within the Roman Church a sincere desire for reform. On the initiative of Contarini a compromise with the Protestants was sought. This attempt at reconciliation failed at the Diet of Ratisbon in 1540. Henceforth in the reform movement within the Roman Church it was the hard line against the Protestants that prevailed. In 1540 Paul II approved the Jesuit Order. The inquisition was re-established in 1542, and in 1545 began the Council of Trent.

Artists in Italy were now affected as much as those in Germany by the course of events within the Church. They turned away from humanism. Michelangelo, who had been influenced in his youth by the appeals of Savonarola, now joined the movement of Contarini. Commissioned by Clement VII, Michelangelo painted a fresco above the altar of the Sistine Chapel between 1534 and 1541. The subject was the Last Judgement, but the spirit of the work was very different from that of the ceiling he had painted a quarter of a century earlier. Like Contarini's movement, it was a compromise. Although he had again become religious, Michelangelo was unable to shed his Neoplatonism entirely. The vicissitudes of his *Last Judgement* reflect the changing attitude of Rome towards the interpretation of religious themes by artists. The reformers in the Curia attacked the fresco because it was likely to draw Protestant fire. Even before he had finished, Michelangelo had to face the reproach of indecency, from a master of ceremonies. Vasari tells us that

> he had already done three-quarters of the work when Pope Paul came to see him. Messer Biagio da Cesena, master of ceremonies and a punctilious person who was in the Chapel with the Pope, on being asked what he

thought of it, said it was a most improper thing to have made in so honourable a place, all these nude figures showing their pudenda so indecently, and that it was not a work for the chapel of the Pope but for baths and taverns. ...

This displeased Michelangelo. Wanting to revenge himself, he painted him from life as soon as he had left, without having him present again, in the shape of Minos with a large serpent coiled round his legs in the midst of a heap of devils. Nor were the entreaties of Messer Biagio, both to the Pope and to Michelangelo, to have this removed of any avail. Michelangelo left it in memory of the incident, and it can still be seen.[15]

Michelangelo was still the divine Michelangelo, offhand with the popes, a law unto himself, above common humanity. But not for long. He was soon to be reduced to a human scale. He was great because the period that had formed him was great. But one is never greater than one's age, and Michelangelo was to suffer the fate of living on into an age that was no longer his own.

The irony was all the more cruel in that he understood the aims of the Counter-Reformation, approved of them and wanted to take part in their realization. But he could not. Driven to despair, in the last years of his life he practically stopped carving and painting. He abandoned art for religion – he tells of this in one of his poems. He thus joined the great iconoclasts. The man whom the world of art venerates as the archetypal artist was rejecting art:

The course of my life across a stormy sea in a fragile bark has already reached the common port where one goes to render account for every action, evil and good. I now know full well how the fond fantasy that made art my idol and my monarch, was burdened with error and with what men desire in their own despite. The thoughts of love, though vain and pleasurable, what are they now as I approach a twofold death? Of one I am certain and the other menaces me. Neither painting nor sculpture can set the soul at rest any more, turned as it is towards that divine love which opens its arms on the Cross in order to enfold us.[16]

A confession like this goes some way to explain Michelangelo's silence when Paul IV wanted to have his fresco destroyed. He said nothing when, in 1559, the Pope ordered Daniele da Volterra, a pupil of Michelangelo's who earned for himself the nickname *il braghettone* (fly), to cover some of the nudes of the *Last Judgement*. In 1566 Pius V had more nudes covered. And in 1596 Clement VIII, tired of half measures, decided to have the whole fresco obliterated; only a plea from the Accademia di San Luca stopped him. In the eighteenth century Clement XIII added still more draperies and in 1936 Pius XI was rumoured to be planning to take up where his predecessors had left off.

In the year of Michelangelo's death, 1564, the theologian Gilio da Fabriano published his *Dialogue on the errors of painters*, supporting and clarifying the directives laid down by the Council of Trent on the subject of painting. The *Last Judgement* came in for serious criticism: Michelangelo had represented the angels without wings; Christ was shown standing, whereas he should have been sitting on his throne of glory; the draperies of some of the figures were blowing in the wind, whereas on the Day of Judgement the wind ought to have stopped blowing.

As its struggle against the Reformation developed, Rome decided to use art as a means of action against Protestant heresy. The result was propagandist art, a concept the leaders of the Soviet Union were to make their own four centuries later. Artists were to be indoctrinated, and their work painstakingly supervised. Recalcitrants would have to answer to the Inquisition.

The Church began by banishing the nude from religious works – we have seen what happened to Michelangelo's *Last Judgement*. Under the influence of the sermons of his day, the sculptor Bartolommeo Ammanati was seized with remorse for those nudes which he had carved in his youth and which he could no longer destroy. In 1582 he wrote to the Academy in Florence to express his repentance. But it was tacitly agreed between the Church and the artist that the legends and mythology of antiquity would remain the chosen field of the nude.

From now on what mattered in a religious painting was that nothing must distract the onlooker from the subject. Nothing must distract the Christian's attention from the mysteries of salvation. Anything that did not contribute to this end must be eliminated. The consequences of this imperative for the future of Western painting were considerable. Landscape, which had gradually become more important in religious scenes, was now deliberately excluded. It became a separate type of painting, as did the domestic interior and the still life. There was henceforth to be a clear dividing line between religious and secular art.

A painter composing a religious work must treat scriptural figures with nobility, on pain of seeing it refused or having to paint it again. Thus a picture by Caravaggio, representing the *Virgin and Child crushing the Serpent*, intended for an altar in St Peter's, was disallowed on the ground that the 'scene was represented in a base manner'. The Church also obliged Caravaggio to paint his St Matthew again because the Saint 'made a vulgar display of his feet'.

On 18 July 1573 Paolo Veronese was summoned to appear before the Holy Office in Venice to answer questions concerning his *Last Supper*. Veronese had continued to paint religious subjects for convents just as if the Reformation and the Counter-Reformation had never happened. He ignored the instructions of the Council of Trent. Into his picture, which should have been confined to Christ and the Apostles, he introduced all kinds of human and animal figures – German pikemen, servants, dwarfs, fools, parrots – all of which the Holy Office considered incompatible with the gravity of the subject and likely to provide the heretics with ammunition.

    Inquisitor: Does it seem to you proper in a painting of the Last Supper of our Lord to represent fools, drunken Germans, dwarfs and other trifles?

    Veronese: No.

    Inquisitor: Why did you do it?

    Veronese: I did it with the idea that these people were outside the room where the supper was taking place.

    Inquisitor: Do you not know that in Germany and

other places infected with heresy they are in the habit of using various paintings full of low subjects and similar inventions to tear to pieces, vilify and make fun of the things of the Holy Catholic Church, in order to teach false doctrine to foolish and ignorant people?

Veronese tried to justify himself: 'The commission was to decorate the picture as I thought fit. It is large and can hold many figures. ... If there is space left in a picture I decorate it with invented figures. ... We painters claim the licence that poets and madmen claim.'

But the inquisitors were not satisfied with Veronese's explanations and ruled that he must correct and amend his picture: 'These things having been transacted, the Lords decreed that the above-mentioned Paolo was bound and obliged to correct and amend the picture within three months to be counted from the day on which the correction to be made was imposed, to be counted at the discretion of the Holy Tribunal, the expenses to be borne by him.'[17]

Veronese did not 'amend' his picture. He changed the title. The *Last Supper* became *The Feast in the House of Levi*.

The Inquisition supervised artists not only to ensure decency and dignity in the representation of religious subjects but also to see to it that they did not introduce, in the words of the Council of Trent, any 'image based on false doctrine'.

If Caravaggio was difficult and Veronese had to be summoned before the Inquisition, the Carracci turned out to be artists after the Church's own heart, creating sacred characters with noble and pious looks, and surrounded by symbols easy for the ordinary people to understand – crosses, haloes, lilies, skulls. The historical importance of the Carracci is immense, since they are at the very origin of modern 'devotional' art, 'the art of Saint-Sulpice', which is today scorned by many Catholic intellectuals on grounds of taste. Yet this despised art contributed to the success of the Counter-Reformation and helped to keep within the orbit of Rome millions of Christians to whose sensibility these images were attuned. The Catholic who condemns these images in the name of 'good taste' should rather consider the question of their religious efficacy. The criterion of taste belongs not to his religion but to the religion of Art.

The Jesuits who took so active a part in the decisions of the Council of Trent were to use art as an instrument of policy. In order to prepare the young missionaries who were sent out to reconquer the Prostestant countries for the Catholic faith, the Jesuits commissioned artists to paint scenes of torture that would familiarize these young men with the idea of death. The Jesuits believed that the daily contemplation of such scenes took away their power to shock, and this point of view was widely held.

Cardinal Paleotti wrote in 1594:

We see every day the most atrocious torments of the saints being represented, and the wheels and the blades and the grids and the chimney hoods and the grills and the wooden horses and the crosses being accurately rendered. The Catholic Church has approved of these being placed before the eyes of the Christian people as heroic emblems of the patience, of the greatness of soul of the holy martyrs, our zealous mother wishing her sons to take courage from these examples and to learn contempt of life if such things should happen to them in the service of God.[18]

For the English College in Rome, where novices were trained for their dangerous mission in heretical England, the Jesuits commissioned Pomarancio to paint a series of frescoes narrating the history of England almost entirely in terms of mutilations and deaths: 'St Edmund being pierced with arrows by the Danes, St Edward and St Thomas of Canterbury being assassinated, St Ebbe and her nuns slitting their noses and mouths to horrify the Vikings and escape violation ... priests being quartered, the faithful dragged to execution, or wrapped up in animal skins and set upon by dogs.'[19] Other paintings in the English College included the sufferings and deaths of forty former pupils who ended as martyrs in England.

Jesuit patronage extended to the greatest artists of the day. Rubens painted for them the *Martyrdom of St Livinus* in which he represented the executioners tearing out the bishop's tongue and throwing it still dripping with blood to a dog. For the Jesuit church in Antwerp, Rubens painted thirty-nine panels 'in accordance', the contract says, 'with the list provided by the Superior'.

Artists did not merely serve the political purposes of the Jesuits and the Counter-Reformation in terms of iconography. The Roman Church followed a policy diametrically opposed to that of the Reformation and decided to counter the austerity of the Protestants with a splendour that appealed to the senses. The Jesuits commissioned artists to cover their churches with marbles, lapis lazuli, bronze and gold in order to make places of worship attractive to the mass of the Faithful. This policy of sumptuousness was held to be justified because as Molanus wrote:

> The temple of God is a figure and an image of the heavens, so that what is found in Christian temples should correspond to what is found in Heaven. ... Let the Christian reflect that when he enters the temple he is entering a kind of heaven on earth where God fills the entire house so that the glory of the Lord may appear to all the multitude, and where the saints are present ... and do not object to anything they see represented in holy images.[20]

The works of the Counter-Reformation with their appeal to emotions and feelings were intended for the masses, unlike those of the Renaissance which appealed to the intellect and had, in fact, a limited, élite public.

By mobilizing artists for the propagation of the Faith once more, the Church reintegrated them in society. They lost their freedom, but until the advent of Romanticism there was to be no bohemian living, no maladjustment, no living outside the law. Artists were no longer gods or demi-gods. When the painter Federigo Zucchari founded an academy in Rome in 1593, modelled on that of Florence but promoted by the Church, his guidelines were conformism and obedience to superiors. And in the following century leading artists like Rubens, Bernini, Velasquez, and Lebrun, all practising Catholics, fell in with the ideology of the ruling class they served.

6 □ The artist as civil servant

The promotion of painters and sculptors from the ranks of the Mechanical Arts, and their metamorphosis into 'Artists' occurred in Italy between the fourteenth and the sixteenth centuries. The other European countries had no part in this process until the seventeenth century, when France superseded Italy as the scene of new developments.

In order to secure its hold in France and spread its ascendancy abroad, the absolute monarchy set out to harness the entire resources of the kingdom to its policies. The monarchy intervened in every aspect of public life – legislation, administration, trade, industry, religion, literature, and also art.

For Louis XIV, art was an instrument of policy. The building of Versailles was a political act. Art was expected to contribute to the splendour of the court, to enhance the prestige of the monarchy, and to develop the myth of royalty. Art had to glorify the State in the person of Louis XIV, the 'Sun King', who had declared '*L'Etat c'est moi*'.

Consequently, artists were regimented and indoctrinated; like soldiers, they were to serve the State with blind obedience. They must submit to the yoke of authority and restrain their individual inspiration and imagination from venturing along paths which it would be against the public interest for them to follow. Artists thus became civil servants, bound by regulations and debarred from undertaking anything not in accordance with the royal will. In order to mobilize artists in favour of the King's personal rule and turn them into civil servants, or government officials, prepared to sacrifice their individuality, the French monarchy drew inspiration from – and perfected – the academy system, as it had been developed by the authoritarian regime of the Dukes of Tuscany and by the Counter-Reformation in Rome.

The 'Académie Royale de Peinture et de Sculpture' – the two Fine Arts as they now began to be called in contradistinction to the mechanical or low Arts – was founded in 1648. It was given a strongly hierarchical structure – there were 'pupils', 'approved pupils', academicians, assistants to professors, professors, rectors, a chancellor, and, at the apex of the pyramid, the vice-protector and the protector. The purpose of the Academy was to mould the artistic personality of painters and sculptors to a uniform pattern. The result of this strict academic discipline was one of the most admired artistic ensembles in the world: Versailles.

Colbert, 'Commandeur et Grand Trésorier des Ordres de Sa Majesté, Contrôleur Général des Finances, Surintendant et Ordonnateur Général des bastiments, arts et manufactures de France', a man trusted by the King, watched closely over the activities of the Academy whose vice-protector he became in 1661. If he was unable to attend himself when the academicians were discussing a political doctrine of art he would delegate two of his officials, Du Metz and Perrault, as reporters. Le Brun, First Painter to the King, was Chancellor of the Academy. As the spokesman of Colbert and of absolutism, he asserted in his lectures the superiority of drawing over colour and of reason over emotion. Colbert wanted Le Brun's and other academicians' painting to be an effective means of royalist propaganda. As the academicians were civil servants paid by the State, it was a cogent demand. On one occasion Louis XIV, addressing a group of influential members of the Academy, declared to them: 'I am entrusting you with my most precious earthly possession ... my glory.'

The statutes of the Academy provided that: 'Each year on 17 October, the eve of the Feast of St Luke, the Academy shall set a general subject on the heroic actions of the King for all students, each to make a drawing of it.'[1]

Two possibilities were open to the artist intending to celebrate the deeds of the monarch: the painting of contemporary history or 'the presentation of modern events in the guise of

Antiquity'. Le Brun inclined towards the later but under Colbert's pressure produced more direct propaganda. He designed and supervised the execution, at the Gobelins, of a series of tapestries narrating the life of Louis XIV – the coronation at Rheims, the visit to the Gobelins, the defeat of the Turks on the Raab, and so on.

The primacy given for political reasons to historical subjects led to the establishment of a hierarchy of genres descending from history painting through portrait, landscape, and animal painting to still life. 'The academic school teaches only history painting; its pupils descend sometimes to the portrait or landscape but these are called historical portrait or historical landscape.'

Félibien, whose influence on generations of artists was to be profound, wrote in the preface to his *Conférences de l'Académie* for 1667:

The painter of perfect landscapes is superior to the one who paints only fruit, flowers or sea shells. The painter of living animals is more estimable than those who represent only things that are dead and without movement. ... It is certain that the painter who imitates God by painting human figures is much more excellent than all the others. ... Nonetheless a painter who only does portraits has not yet achieved the high perfection of the art. To achieve it he must pass from one figure to the representation of several together; he must treat history and fable; he must represent great actions as historians do; or agreeable subjects as do poets; and, rising yet higher, he must know by having recourse to allegorical compositions how to cover with the veil of fable the virtues of great men and the most sublime mysteries.[2]

Today, art historians and connoisseurs tend on the whole to be condescending towards Félibien and his hierarchy of genres and to consider history paintings with contempt or indifference. They seem to forget the central place occupied by historical scenes on the walls and ceilings of Versailles. Foreign diplomats entering Le Vau's Versailles were greeted by the vanquished emblems of Spain and the Empire. They found them again painted on the vault of the Grand Escalier. 'The Dutch War, the Passage of the Rhine, Europe apparently subdued proclaim the glory of the King in the ceiling of Mansart's and Le Brun's gallery or in the grove of the Triumphal Arch.'[3]

But according to Saint-Simon, these emphatic statements intended to impress foreign visitors had a harmful effect on the absolute monarchy: 'the magnificent history paintings [by Mignard] that decorate the Grande Galerie at Versailles and its Salons have had no small part in irritating Europe against the King and making her join forces against his person even more than against his kingdom'.[4] Saint-Simon denounces not only the dangers of art and its boomerang effect but the expenses incurred for Versailles, by a king drunk with prestige and glory: 'As neither he [Mansart] nor the King had any taste, nothing beautiful or even convenient was ever made with these immense sums. ... This chapel at Versailles, fine in point of workmanship and decoration which has cost so many millions and so many years.'[5]

Colbert also condemned the waste; he wrote to the King: 'If Your Majesty wants to search Versailles for the 500,000 écus and more spent there in the last two years, Your Majesty will have difficulty in finding them.'[6] The costs of this monument erected by a despot's folly were dear not only in money but also in men. Workmen were killed on the scaffoldings. When the mother of one of these, killed at the *machines de Versailles*, dared to speak her mind about the 'Roi Soleil', he had her arrested and whipped. Versailles helped to increase the royal deficit as well as the widespread poverty and monetary inflation that characterized the last years of the reign of Louis XIV. Those who claim that this has been made good in our time by the inflow of foreign exchange and the prestige of Versailles are simply offering proof of their own blindness.

To design and carry through the vast and costly work at Versailles Louis XIV found in the person of his First Painter, Le Brun, an orchestrator of calibre, worthy of his ambition. Charles Le Brun – whom the King raised to the nobility in 1662 by letters patent couched in extremely flattering terms, as a reward for his devotion to the cause of absolute monarchy – was born on 24 February 1619 into a modest family engaged in the Mechanical Arts. His father was a master sculptor, his godfather a master mason. By his energy Le Brun not only contributed to the elevation of painters and sculptors in France above the Mechanical Arts; his lectures and his other activities mark a stage in the evolution of the religion of Art. In this respect he is a landmark in the history of art comparable to Ghiberti, Alberti, Ficino, or Michelangelo. The seventeenth-century painters like Rubens, Velasquez, Rembrandt or Vermeer, who are much better known today than Le Brun, played little or no part in the history of ideas.

When Le Brun was serving his apprenticeship in the first half of the seventeenth century, painters and sculptors in France had not yet been transformed into artists like their colleagues in Italy. They were still artisans or workmen, the two words being at the time almost synonymous. Their social standing was therefore low. The jurist Loyseau in his *Traité des Ordres et simples dignités* (1613) speaks of them with contempt: 'We commonly call mechanical what is low and mean.'[7] Loyseau did not think that artisans, men of the Mechanical Arts, belonged to the bourgeoisie or Third Estate. The criterion was manual labour.

When French painters looked towards Italy they noted with envy that south of the Alps painters were no longer despised as artisans or manual workers. But in France there was as yet no basis for a comparable development. Only privileged individuals succeeded in breaking away from the corporations by becoming painter to the king or to the queen with the honorific title of *valet de chambre*. In the seventeenth century they were called *brevetaires* (literally 'patentees').

No wonder, then, that from the middle of the sixteenth century onwards it became customary for French painters to go to Rome or elsewhere in Italy to enjoy the esteem they considered their due. Some stayed for only a short time, others for longer spells, like Nicolas Poussin (from 1624 to 1640 and from 1642 to 1649), or Claude Gellée, called 'Le Lorrain', who stayed for fifty-five years. Yet others settled down for good like Giovanni da Bologna, whose original name was Jean de Douai, or Mola di Francia, the italianized Jean-Baptiste Mole.

There was also an Italian phase in Le Brun's career. In 1642 he arrived in Rome and, like many other foreign painters, was elected to the Accademia di San Luca which had been founded by Zucchari at the end of the previous century. He thus had an opportunity of observing from inside the functioning of an academy, and the advantages it could offer not only to the painter but also to the State.

Shortly after Le Brun's return to Paris the Communauté des métiers de Paris protested against the privileges of the *brevetaires* and asked the Parlement to limit their number. The *brevetaires* took alarm and, under Le Brun's leadership, submitted to the King, through the intermediary of a connoisseur nobleman, M. de Charmois, a request for the foundation of an academy.

One finds in this request, dated 20 January 1648, the same arguments as those put forward in the fifteenth and sixteenth centuries to release painters and sculptors from the Mechanical Arts in which they have been 'unjustly placed':

Painting and sculpture had at all times a honourable place among the Greeks and Romans, and were professed freely and nobly. ... In France these two fine arts have for several centuries been in a state of extreme abasement, exposed to the shame of a overlordship that degraded them; subjected to a gang of ignorant and grasping jurors, low artisans without elevation or merit.[8]

The 'Noble Arts' must be separated from the 'Mechanical Arts'.

The request, which was granted – the foundation meeting of the Académie Royale de Peinture et de Sculpture took place on 1 February following – is of especial interest for our purpose as it offers the earliest instance, to our knowledge, of the term 'beaux Arts' written with a small 'b' and a capital 'A'. To the author or authors (Le Brun and several other *brevetaires* took part in the drafting) of the document, painting and sculpture were Liberal Arts for which they invented the name 'beaux Arts' (fine arts). Later this became 'Beaux-Arts' with a capital 'B' and a hyphen, and, having hardened into a technical term, ousted the term 'Arts liberaux' which means very little today to the educated Frenchman.

Henceforth the terms 'Arts' and 'Beaux-Arts' began to be used indiscriminately. The other manual skills continued to be considered as the occupations of workmen or artisans in the traditional way. In the second half of the seventeenth century Félibien still used the word *ouvrier* with reference to painters and sculptors.

In order to accentuate the difference between artists and artisans the teaching at the Academy favoured theory at the expense of technique. The idea was to show that for the artist the 'hand is the servant of the mind', that painting is, as Leonardo had called it, 'cosa mentale'. The Academy was a school that taught geometry, perspective and anatomy; there was drawing from live models but no actual painting or carving was done on the premises. A large part of the curriculum consisted of lectures given by the principal academicians; these included discussions about the merits of celebrated pictures by Raphael or Poussin. This teaching, which was closely supervised by the monarchy, especially after 1661 when Louis XIV began to rule in person, was intended to supply the State with artists capable of directing the workmen in the royal industries, or *'manufactures'* as they were then called, in accordance with the wishes of the monarchy. The Academy thus became a training centre for the young painters and sculptors who were needed for the King's buildings.

In 1663 Colbert appointed Le Brun director of the *manufacture* he had just established at the Gobelins, which was intended to produce furnishings for Versailles and the other royal residences. And Le Brun, the painter-civil servant, was to leave his mark on all the various standardized artefacts produced at the Gobelins – furniture, bronzes, tapestry and silver plate.

To make the artists toe the royal line the Academy could use many pressures and inducements. Not only was it their paymaster but it also distributed prizes, like the *prix de Rome* which offered artists the opportunity to stay at the Académie de France in Rome, founded as a branch of the Paris Academy in 1666. The Academy awarded royal commissions; it could confer titles and grant pensions. It also provided facilities for exhibiting in public – the celebrated Salons, so important for artists in the eighteenth and nineteenth centuries, evolved out of this.

To be an academician and a civil servant was a privilege. It meant security of employment, or so it seemed. It meant keeping one's social distance from the 'rude mechanicals'. It meant a place of honour at the court of the most powerful monarch in Europe. Only a few old-fashioned nobles dared to continue addressing artists familiarly like workmen. But to be an academician meant also selling one's soul and linking one's fate with that of a political regime that was, to say the least, authoritarian. It meant bartering one's freedom for security and honours, like those painters and sculptors whom Vasari had trained a century earlier in his Academy in Florence.

But towards the end of the century the economic basis of this security and full employment began to crumble. The combined burden of ever longer wars and court ostentation was ruining the country's finances. In an attempt to make up for the national deficit, Louis XIV increased taxes. In 1689, two months before Le Brun's death, he decided to have the royal silver (which his First Painter had designed) melted down, and he also considerably reduced the expenditure on Versailles. That year the building budget was lowered from 7 to 1.5 million.

The artists of the Academy were among the first to be affected by these cuts in the sums allowed for the royal buildings. In 1694 their situation worsened sharply. A series of austerity measures decreed by the King included the temporary closing of the Academy. This deprived the artists of their salaries as government servants. Thus, within a few years the artists of the Academy, having been comfortably off if not rich, having known security and the prestige that went with their new status as senior government servants playing an active role in the political life of the State, found themselves toppled from their pedestals and exposed to the hazards of the open market, and the uncertainty of the struggle for survival. It was a situation that was to lead them at the time of Romanticism to become once more the artists at odds with society, which Italy had already seen before the Counter-Reformation.

7 □ The artist, dealer and critic

Unlike those in France, artists in Holland had already found themselves at the mercy of the open market from the beginning of the seventeenth century. There was no institutional framework comparable to the system of Louis XIV or of the Medicis in Florence in which to accommodate them. There was no central power interested in founding an academy in order to satisfy its political ambition. Holland was a middle-class republic averse to ostentation, luxury and prestige-spending. The artists were to suffer accordingly – but no matter! A democratic regime is preferable to an absolute monarchy.

Not only were there no State commissions; there were no Church commissions either. No altar pieces or frescoes were needed. This political and religious situation, peculiar to Protestant Holland in the seventeenth century, produced absolutely anarchic working conditions for painters, conditions which in many ways foreshadowed those we know and suffer from today in the Western world – and for the same reasons.

In the absence of regular commissions – those from corporations and civic bodies were relatively few and infrequent – Dutch painters of the period produced unsolicited works in their own studios, a new phenomenon, the economic consequence of which was to upset the balance between supply and demand and introduce the risk of overproduction and depreciation. We use this terminology advisedly: under such circumstances, whether we like it or not, paintings can only become commodities, subject to the laws of the market.

With trade as the national pursuit, Dutch burghers had no inhibitions about treating pictures like any other sort of merchandise. The Italian notion of the work of art as an object *sui generis* had not yet reached the Low Countries.

Holland was enjoying a monetary surplus, and not only was there trade in pictures but also speculation in them. The taste for speculation grew in spite of occasional setbacks like the *tulipomania*, one of the most extraordinary stories of speculation of all time. In the 1630s tulip bulbs were negotiated like shares, quoted on the stock exchange, and had due dates. A tulip bulb was at one stage worth twelve acres of land. All classes of society were infected by the fever of speculation, until one day the market collapsed.

When John Evelyn, the English diarist, was passing through Rotterdam he commented on this spirit of speculation and the profits made even by simple farmers, from the purchase and sale of pictures:

> We arrived late at Rotterdam, where was ... their annual Marte or Faire, so furnished with pictures ... that I was amazed. ... The reason for this store of pictures and their cheapness proceeds from their want of Land, to employ their Stock; so as 'tis an ordinary thing to find a common Farmer lay out two or 3,000 pounds in this commodity, their houses are full of them, and they vend them at their Kermas'es to very greate gaines.[1]

It was this ambition of burghers and well-to-do farmers to acquire pictures as a commercial proposition or to imitate those higher up in the social scale, or indeed, one must admit, to decorate their houses, that brought about an inflationary situation in painting. The market was soon saturated and painters were obliged to accept ridiculously low prices for their work. Jan Steen at the height of his career had to content himself with 27 gulden for three portraits, while Isaak van Ostade was obliged to supply his dealer with thirteen pictures for the same sum. An ox at that time fetched 90 gulden.

There was only one thing painters could do in order to survive and that was to find a second means of livelihood. Jan van Goyen became an estate agent, Hobbema a tax-collector, Jan Steen an innkeeper, Ruisdael a barber-surgeon. Some set up as dealers in their own works or in those of others – selling paintings, drawings or etchings. Among them were Vermeer and Rembrandt. The latter was very active in this field at the beginning of his career.

Beside these painter-dealers, there emerged in the Low Countries in the seventeenth century a mass of professional art dealers called forth by the painters' need to dispose of their pictures. They were soon a major force in the market and, acting as intermediaries between the painter and the public, influenced the behaviour and outlook of both. They managed to broaden the gulf between the two and to isolate the artist, and are therefore to a certain extent responsible for the gap which separates the modern artist from the public.

As in our own day, dealers took up particular artists and sometimes made them sign exclusive contracts in which the artist undertook to hand over everything he painted to the dealer. Thus in 1647 a one-year contract was made between the dealer Bartholomeus Floquet and the painter Elias van den Broech. The artist was to receive a lodging subsidy of 39 gulden, and be fed, and he was to be paid an annual salary of 120 gulden, in consideration for which he was to be available at all times to paint for Floquet any subject that the dealer's commercial imagination might suggest. It was also specified that if the painter was absent for a day or got married he must pay 'damages' to the dealer.

What is significant in this contract is that it is the dealer who dictates the subjects to be painted. In fact the subjects he commissioned would be those that the public asked for and bought in his shop.

In spite of the efforts of dealers to control the market in this way, it deteriorated. Painters not controlled by dealers produced too much. Inside Holland the market was saturated and the possibilities for exporting Dutch paintings were limited. Prices and profits fell. This situation led many dealers to give up contemporary painting and concentrate on old masters, which meant a further slump in value for the former. A few centuries later, Lord Duveen was to act similarly.

These seventeenth-century dealers had by and large a bad reputation. They were sometimes associated with the shadier type of middleman. A well-known Amsterdam dealer, Jan

Pieters Zoomer, who put famous names to the work of indifferent painters was ironically known as 'John-the-Baptist-in-Art'. There were numerous instances of copies being sold as originals.

Before long, the market in old masters was in decline as well, affected by the war and the adverse economic conditions. In 1655 the government cut the interest on its debts from 5 to 4 per cent. The economic crisis made life still more difficult for artists – sometimes desperate. Money was scarce for there was no longer any surplus. Few people bought pictures. Rembrandt went bankrupt and the small number of Vermeer's paintings is traceable perhaps to economic causes. When Vermeer died, his widow faced bankruptcy. She declared before the bankruptcy court: 'During the recent war against the King of France [my] husband ... was able to earn little or nothing. Moreover, in order to pay for the keep of his ... children, he was forced to part at great loss with the works of art he had purchased and in which he traded.'[2]

The contemporary situation in France was rather different. There existed an active market in paintings, more or less in the shadow of the Academy but markedly different from that in Holland. It was confined to a limited number of interested individuals or connoisseurs recruited from the country's ruling class. It was a market for an élite – or for people who considered themselves as such. It was not dominated by dealers. Under the influence of Italy, modern pictures were regarded as works of art and not as commodities. The painters working for this market were not exposed to hardship, at least not until the economic crisis at the end of the century threw them into disarray as it did those artists who had been working for the State. There were then too many painters working for private patrons.

One of these connoisseurs, Louis-Henri de Loménie, Comte de Brienne, describes himself as follows:

I was born a painter without realizing it and I became a connoisseur by dint of having money. Connoisseurship is practicable only for prodigals like myself or for kings who can afford such outlays without inconvenience. But for private individuals it is certainly a great folly and the expense involved is infinitely beyond their means. ... I have spent a great deal of money on pictures.³

Too much money, in fact. For Louis-Henri de Loménie himself spent beyond his means. He inherited from his father the office of Secretary of State, but his collection of paintings involved him in such expense that he took to gambling and fraud. He was caught, exiled and deprived of his office (1663). Accused subsequently of further malpractices he was sent by his family to S. Lazare, part lunatic asylum, part approved school. He remained there for eighteen years during which he wrote his memoirs, an invaluable source of information on the Paris picture market in the seventeenth century. Even Loménie, wary as he was of dealers, was sometimes tricked by them. Nevertheless he boasts: 'I know my way about pictures. I can buy one without taking anybody's advice and without fear of being cheated by the Jabachs and the Perruchots, the Forests and the potentates, great jobbers of pictures who have in their time sold copies for originals.'⁴

But further on in his memoirs Loménie de Brienne forgets what he has written before and admits to being cheated on three occasions by the forgers. Once when he bought a 'fine copy of a Poussin', another time when he acquired a 'fine Virgin by Domenichino ... which Forest guaranteed as original'. On the third occasion he was cheated again but he got his own back:

> Michelin sold me for an original a fine copy by Forest which I took to be a Mola. But this could easily happen and must not be held against an apprentice connoisseur who did not know at the time what Forest was capable of. But I cheated the cheater. I had Forest copy my little Mola *Agar* for 100 *livres* and sold it to Michelin, the botcher of pictures, as an original for 400.⁵

Louis Hourticq, relating this anecdote in his *De Poussin à Watteau*, adds: 'A little *Agar* by Mola is now at the Louvre, no doubt the one that belonged to Brienne. Let us hope it is not the copy by Forest!'⁶

Let us hope there were not too many copies in Brienne's

collection, for some of the celebrated Raphaels, Titians, Veroneses and Poussins that the public admire at the Louvre belonged at one stage to the Secretary of State.

Brienne collected mainly old masters but he also dealt in some contemporary painters like Poussin. Poussin was the one painter who was a good buy in his own lifetime. He thrilled the connoisseurs. When a painting by him was announced from Italy they would rush to be present at the unwrapping and give their opinions. Poussins were already expensive and there were complaints about this. Louis de Fouquet, writing from Rome to his brother, the Surintendant, who was trying to acquire some Poussins, speaks of the 'dearness' – two hundred pistoles each: 'It would be more to one's profit to get him [Poussin] to paint some pictures than to buy those already painted. His works some time after his death will be a thousand times rarer and more expensive.'[7] And indeed Poussins were soon selling at five times their earlier price. Brienne records that M. de Seignelay, Colbert's son, 'gave a thousand pistoles for the little *Moses* which I had bought for not more than two thousand francs.'[8]

This craze for Poussin was a stimulus to forgers who inundated the Rome and Paris markets with fakes. Connoisseurs were understandably worried. Whenever possible they asked the artist to authenticate his paintings as is done today. M. de Monconys, having bought a Poussin in Rome, rushed to see the artist: 'I was at the Piazza di Spagna to see M. Poussin who recognized and vouched for the picture of Narcissus that I had by him.'[9]

Poussin was launched by Roman connoisseurs, especially Cassiano del Pozzo, a celebrated collector who is said to have possessed as many as fifty of his canvasses. When his reputation reached Paris, Richelieu recalled him to direct work on the Louvre. It was a failure. Poussin, indifferent to politics and incapable of supervising workmen, used the excuse of his wife's illness to return to Rome and stay there for good. He returned to his easel and from then on worked only for Roman and Parisian connoisseurs, who were like himself often indifferent to politics. The subjects they commissioned, mainly from ancient history or mythology, had no connection with contemporary events but furnished examples for the contemplation and discussion of beauty.

One of the most celebrated seventeenth-century connoisseurs in France (he was to own, among others, Poussin's *Inspiration of the Poet*, now in the Louvre) was an Italian of extremely modest family background, Mazarin, Richelieu's successor at the head of the country. The chief motive that led him to collect works of art with such frenzy was not a love of meditation but the secret ambition to make people forget his humble origins. In this he imitated the Medici and anticipated the Rothschilds. Loménie de Brienne, who was his private secretary, tells how, shortly before his death, Mazarin walking about in his gallery said: 'Ah, my poor friend, the time has come to leave all this. Farewell dear pictures which I have loved, and which have cost me, so much.'[10] In fact the money Mazarin had laid out was not his own but the taxpayers'. And this disreputable practice was imitated by many superintendents of finances who came after him. Some of the collections that are the pride of French museums were thus put together with misappropriated funds.

For other people, who had no qualms about their social origins, like the nobility, buying pictures was a way of rapidly appreciating their patrimony. The marquis de Coulanges wrote in 1675 to Madame de Sevigné: 'Pictures are as good as gold bars, there has never been a better investment. You will always get double for them if you want to sell. Do not worry about the new ones you have acquired for Grignan and decorate your courts and forecourts with them when you have enough in your rooms.'[11]

Even Louis XIV was aware of the possibilities of the picture market. Like the Abbé Louis de Fouquet, he knew that works by contemporary painters would increase in value after the artist's death. One day the King came to the defence of Le Brun, who was under attack from a group of connoisseurs who objected to his large historical compositions and criticized the quality of his easel painting. 'After Monsieur Le Brun's death,' Louis declared to the Dauphine in the painter's presence, 'these pictures will be priceless.' Then turning to Le Brun: 'However, Monsieur Le Brun, you must not die of hunger to gain recognition for your work, I value it already without your having to do that.'[12] Nevertheless, to justify his high reputation with connoisseurs, Le Brun devoted more of his time in the last years of his life to easel painting.

Following the military defeats of Louis XIV and the economic crisis that hit France at the end of the century, the fate of the academicians began to depend increasingly on the opinion of connoisseurs. When the King found himself obliged to cut back drastically the expenditure on Versailles and his other palaces, the academicians were deprived of their chief source of income. In order to survive they had to adapt themselves and take up easel painting for private patrons.

At this stage the academicians discovered the importance of the public exhibitions which had been started by Colbert and Le Brun in 1667 as a means of establishing contact with prospective buyers. In the eighteenth century the Salon Carré in the Louvre was used for the purpose, and painters were described as exhibiting 'at the Salon'. At different periods exhibitions were held either once or twice a year and lasted about twenty days. A few painters who were not members of the Academy were sometimes invited to exhibit 'at the door' of the Salon. Up to 1748 academicians were free to send any – and as many – pictures as they wished, but in that year a jury was appointed to accept or reject the works presented.

In order to keep in touch with connoisseurs in the provinces and abroad, artists had their pictures engraved. Raphael and other sixteenth-century painters had already done this, and for a similar purpose. According to Vasari, 'This habit and manner of making prints has developed so far that those who make a profession of it keep draughtsmen continually employed; these copy whatever beautiful work has just been made and make a print of it.'[13] In the eighteenth century artists often organized their own publicity by having prints made in advance of the pictures they intended to exhibit at the next Salon, in order to arouse the curiosity of the collectors.

There were other Salons in Paris in the eighteenth century –

the Salon de la Correspondance, and the Salon de la Jeunesse
– though it was beneath the dignity of academicians to exhibit
in them. The most celebrated was the one held on Corpus
Christi day in the Place Dauphine, in the open air, as part of a
kind of fair, and in which young and unknown artists could
exhibit. It was there that Chardin, exhibiting his *Rayfish*
(today in the Louvre), was discovered and invited to present
himself before the Academy. The Colisée, a place of music-
hall type entertainment, began to run picture exhibitions.
They were a success, much to the horror of the Academy,
which had them prohibited.

The Academy Salon was the one most highly regarded.
Entry was free of charge and it attracted large crowds. Collectors were becoming more and more numerous. And a lay
public composed of nobles, members of the bourgeoisie and
servants flocked to look at the pictures. There was an element
of snobbery in it – one 'did' the Salon. Titled persons, an-
noyed at having to rub shoulders with lackeys, obtained leave
from the Director of Buildings to come outside opening hours.

At the entrance, a guide (*livret*) – today it would be a
catalogue – was on sale describing, with an introduction, the
works exhibited. The popularity of the Salon may be gauged
from the fact that in one year twenty thousand copies of the
guide were printed. In order to make the visitors buy it, the
pictures were not labelled – a practice not unfamiliar in
present-day exhibitions.

But guides were not enough for the public, which wanted to
know how to form an opinion of what it saw and to understand the reasons for the preferences of the connoisseurs. And
so from 1738 onwards there began to appear booklets or
newspaper articles, anonymous, commenting on the merits of
the works exhibited. Some artists used these reviews as a form
of publicity, arranging for their friends to write favourable
ones; such precautions were doubtless justified, for most of
the criticisms that appeared were harsh. The artists were
vexed and complained to the Director of Buildings and the
police officers. These latter decreed that such articles had to
be signed and submitted to censorship. In 1767 three leading

painters of the day, Boucher, La Tour and Greuze, 'tired of exposing themselves to asses and being torn to pieces by them',[14] withheld their work from the Salon.

The first real art critic was Lafont de Saint-Yenne. In 1746 he published a little book called *Réflexions sur quelques causes de l'état présent de la peinture en France*, followed by an examination of the pictures exhibited in that year's Salon. Art criticism differs from the philosophy of art, in that it discusses the merits of individual works. In order that the works of old and new masters could be judged and compared side by side Lafont de Saint-Yenne suggested the creation of a museum – he did not actually use the word – 'A place set apart for housing permanently the innumerable masterpieces of the greatest masters of Europe'.[15]

But it is with Diderot that art criticism can be said to have come of age. Baron Grimm was running for the benefit of a select circle of crowned heads – the Queen of Sweden, the King of Poland, the Empress of Russia – and other important persons his *Correspondance littéraire* to keep them in touch with Parisian life and letters. In 1759 he asked Diderot to review the Salons; Diderot agreed and went on contributing until 1781. He was one of the very few writers of calibre to write art criticism. From the eighteenth century to our day, art criticism has generally been the stamping ground of failed or second-rate writers who have found in it a field where their imagination is free to roam without their verbosity attracting the strictures of literary criticism.

Diderot undertook his task conscientiously. He went to the Salon on the opening day and on as many more days as was necessary. He often asked artists like Chardin or Falconet to come with him and talk about their work and their views on art. He visited their studios. It must be stressed that Diderot's good relations with his artist friends were exceptional, and remained unimpaired even when he was critical of their work – the *Correspondance littéraire* was not distributed in Paris! He could thus afford to have independent opinions, which has not, alas, been the case with the majority of art critics, past or present. Personal acquaintance with the painters and sculptors they write about has tended to make them blunt the edge of their criticisms for fear of offending the artists' sensibilities.

Like all reformers from Plato to the Fathers assembled at the Council of Trent, Diderot wanted artists to serve a cause, in his case the struggle of the 'philosopher' against the established order. Like earlier reformers, he applied his own moral criteria to works of art, approving some, condemning others. Thus he attacked artists who worked for the decadent nobility, and encouraged those he considered to be contributing to the emancipation of the bourgeoisie.

Reacting against the austerity of the last years of Louis XIV's reign, the nobility plunged into a life of pleasure and debauch. The tone was set by the Regent, who abandoned Versailles for Paris, and a stylized court life for small intimate gatherings. What was wanted now were not great historical frescoes celebrating the glory of the armies but pictures evoking the pleasures of love. François Boucher, the favourite painter of Madame de Pompadour and successor of Charles Le Brun, catered for this licentious taste by painting voluptuous Venuses and Bacchantes. Angels and children are often seen frolicking around these splendid nudes. Speaking for the bourgeoisie, Diderot blamed Boucher not only for filling his pictures with 'nipples and buttocks' but also for always painting frivolous scenes in which nobody does any work. 'When he paints children you will not find one that could be employed in the ordinary affairs of life – studying, reading, writing, stripping hemp.'[16] Diderot wanted painters to represent these 'ordinary affairs of life', and it is not surprising to find him denouncing the whole gamut of mythological subjects so popular with an aristocracy that had little desire to be reminded of the social realities around them. He wanted painting to have a human content, to speak for the misery of the humble against the pride of the mighty, to inspire virtue and purify morals.

Diderot believed that he had found in Greuze the painter he was looking for: one who combined realism with moral preoccupations. Greuze's pictures were painted dramas: *The Return of the Prodigal Son, The Village Betrothal,* or *A Father explaining the Bible to his Children.* Diderot interpreted these paintings as protests against the moral decadence of the nobility. In fact, their message was quite traditional, and both the nobility and the bourgeoisie could be equally moved by the sight of the father explaining the Bible. Greuze was scarcely concerned at all to question the established order which Diderot and his friends were trying to undermine. His *Widow and her Priest* was dedicated to the 'Guardians of Religion and Manners'.

After a time Diderot's developing social and political awareness led him to abandon Greuze and turn his attention to more revolutionary painters like David, who painted subjects from ancient history in which the bourgeoisie could derive inspiration from the example of Roman civic virtue. In 1793 David, a member of the Convention, voted for the death of Louis XVI.

Since aesthetic theory has come to put sensibility before subject matter, Diderot has become unpopular with art historians, who reproach him for singing the praises of Greuze, a painter ill-thought of today and said to have little artistic sense. But such historians are either guilty of bad faith or ignorant of the texts. There are many passages in Diderot which show quite clearly that he was aware of Greuze's weaknesses. Thus in 1759 he wrote: 'The Greuzes are not extraordinary this year. The rendering is stiff and the colour insipid and whitish. They used to appeal to me, I do not care for them any more.'[17] But it is true that the pursuit of political aims could make him indulgent towards defects of this kind. Nevertheless, some passages full of admiration which he devotes to Chardin, whose subjects carried no moral message, give clear evidence of Diderot's artistic sensibility: 'This man is the foremost colourist of the Salon and perhaps one of the foremost colourists of [all] painting.'[18] 'He understands the harmony of colours and reflections. O Chardin! It is not white, red, black that you grind on your palette: it is the very substance of objects, it is air and light that you take on the point of your brush and attach to the canvas.'[19] Diderot's opinion of the respective value of the two painters is not in doubt. Apparently Greuze himself all but conceded as much: 'I was told that Greuze coming up to the Salon and noticing the piece by Chardin I have just described, looked at it and walked on heaving a deep sigh. Such praise is both shorter and worth more than mine.'[20]

His visits to the Salon revealed to Diderot that the bourgeoisie was not as virtuous as he had thought. It was showing its defects even before accomplishing its political revolution. Diderot was very disappointed. The aristocracy was not alone in having vices. There were too many among the bourgeoisie who exploited artists and speculated in works of art. This aroused Diderot's indignation:

This is how the majority of wealthy men who engage artists calculate: 'The money I am going to invest in Boucher's drawings, in Vernet's, Casanova's, Loutherbourg's paintings, will be money put out at the highest interest. I shall have the lifelong enjoyment of an excellent piece. The artist will die; and my children and I will obtain for the piece twenty times its original price.' The calculation is correct and heirs are not sorry to see wealth they covet used in this way.[21]

Diderot's collector calculates like many a twentieth-century parvenu. Grimm wrote that 'buying pictures to resell them is an excellent way of investing one's money'.[22]

The financial crisis of the eighteenth century – notably the South Sea Bubble – drew attention to the financial soundness of works of art. They were not, or not yet, subject to depreciation like money. The great collectors of the century were recruited mainly from the bourgeoisie, in particular financiers, bankers and *fermiers généraux*. These men had ready cash when a picture of value appeared on the market, where a landed proprietor had to go through the time-consuming process of selling land.

But it was not solely the attraction of gain that moved the bourgeois in his passion for the work of art; there was also love of the object, of the thing possessed. This cult of the object was a basic factor in the development of 'taste'. Régine Pernoud writes in her *Histoire de la bourgeoisie en France*:

Bourgeois society came to consider taste and discrimination as the most important qualities, the mark of those who, in the midst of an ever more differentiated society, have been successful and have secured for themselves a position of advantage. An important corollary of the education that such people required for their children was the formation of taste and 'distinguished' habits, which could continue to guarantee the social prestige of the bourgeois at a time when for political reasons acquiring a title would cease to be fashionable. It is in eighteenth-century society that 'taste' achieved this new importance.[23]

As the importance of 'taste' grew, especially during the second half of the century, an ever increasing number of dealers, brokers and middlemen of all kinds bent on exploiting the art market began to mingle with the collectors themselves. Various pamphlets were written to denounce their machinations. Thus at sales, a frequent occurrence at the time, dealers clubbed together, as they do today, to keep the bids down and resell what they had bought by putting it up for auction again. The difference between the two sale prices was shared among the participants.

Dealers and middlemen were always hovering around artists' studios trying to make themselves indispensable. Diderot hit out against them:

It is these people that interpose themselves between the man of wealth and the indigent artist; that make the man of talent pay for the protection they give him; that open and close doors to him; that snatch his best products from him for a measly price; that lie in wait behind his easel; that have secretly condemned him to beggary in order to hold him enslaved and dependent; their constant theme is that a modest income is the necessary stimulus to the artist.[24]

These lines reveal how indigent and how insecure artists could be in a society in which their production was subject to the law of supply and demand. In the last decades that preceded the Revolution their situation was similar to that of the Dutch artists in the seventeenth century – and for similar reasons. Both Church and State in France had given up their role of patrons. The monarchy had been in financial difficulties since the end of Louis XIV's reign and was no longer interested in artistic prestige propaganda on its behalf. It is also true that the more intimate interiors of the eighteenth century, in which wainscotting and mirrors were an important part of the decoration, ruled out vast compositions, and wall paintings had to be skied above doors and mirrors. As for the Church, its commissions for religious paintings had become rare in this age of Enlightenment (there were fewer of them at each year's Salon).

In default of regular commissions from Church or State, the majority of artists found themselves obliged to produce subjects likely to attract buyers who were often anonymous and whose social background varied widely: pretty mythological scenes, pastorals, interiors, or stories with a moral. They lived in the hope that a connoisseur of note would spot their work and rescue them overnight from obscurity and want. However, there was a category of painters who worked by commission and did not have to submit to the whims of buyers or see their work transformed into a market commodity: the portrait painters. The portrait appealed to human vanity, whether King or bourgeois. Portrait painters were much in demand; they lived in security, comfortably off.

Maurice Quentin de la Tour asked the considerable sum of 48,000 *livres* for the portrait of Madame de Pompadour. The scale of this can be judged by comparison with the annual wage of manual workers at the time, which was 260 *livres*. And the painter was doing a favour, as is evident from the tone adopted by the influential M. de Marigny, Superintendent of Buildings and brother of the King's mistress, when he intervened on her behalf: 'May my sister hope to be painted by you?'[25] La Tour agreed on condition that he should not be disturbed during the sittings. An anecdote illustrates La Tour's extraordinary self-assurance. He was starting to paint when Louis XIV came in. 'You promised me, Madame, that your door would be closed.' The King laughed good-naturedly ... and suggested that he should continue. 'It is impossible for me to obey Your Majesty,' the painter replied, 'I shall come back when Madame is alone.' Thereupon he got up ... and went out to dress in another room, repeating several times, 'I cannot abide being interrupted.'[26]

This story and others like it show how, within a century, painters in France rose from the status of manual workers to a position where they treated kings and princes as equals or even with impertinence. La Tour refused to finish pastel portraits of the King's daughters, Mesdames de France, as a punishment for missed appointments. The Dauphine could not obtain her own portrait because she had been rash enough to suggest an alternative place for sitting.

Asked to paint a portrait of the King, La Tour was taken to a room which had light on every side. 'Ah!' he exclaimed, 'what am I supposed to do in this lantern: what is needed for painting is light from one direction only.'

'I chose it for its seclusion,' replied Louis XIV, 'in order not to be disturbed.'

'I did not know, Sire,' the artist rejoined, 'that you were not master in your own house.'[27]

One day, finding the Dauphin not well informed about a matter he had brought to his attention, La Tour said: 'This is how you and your kind always allow yourselves to be deceived by rascals.'[28]

Not since Michelangelo had an artist treated the powers that be with such nonchalance. But Michelangelo had considered himself a demi-god. La Tour claimed to be no more than a simple citizen. The Counter-Reformation had reintegrated artists in society; Romanticism was to exile them from it.

8 □ Towards the religion of the Beautiful

In our chapter on the birth of the Artist we examined the way in which the religion of Art was born in Renaissance Italy. What was the French contribution during the seventeenth and eighteenth centuries to this religion of Art – or of the Beautiful?

In the second half of the seventeenth century it was Frenchmen who began to take over from the Italian theoreticians of art, from Alberti, Ficino, Leonardo, Lomazzo, Zucchari. In the 1660s there appeared in rapid succession several works containing views on the principles of painting, written by French painters or gentlemen connoisseurs. In 1662 Fréart de Chambray brought out his *Idée de la perfection de la peinture démontrée par les principes de l'art*; in 1666 Félibien, the royal historiographer, published the first volume of his *Entretiens*; in 1668 the painter Dufresnoy published his Latin poem *De arte graphica*; and in the same year Charles Perrault, the author of the fairy tales, published his poem *La Peinture*.

But it was at the Academy, where paintings were constantly 'reasoned about' (*raisonnement de la peinture*), that a systematic doctrine of art, of the beautiful or of aesthetics, was being elaborated. The Academy had a programme of lectures followed by discussions. The results of these were intended to be in some sense authoritative: 'It would be proper if the decisions of the Academy were accompanied by a statement of the reasons that lead the Academy to adopt them.'[1] To give more weight and a wider audience to its pronouncements, the Academy decided to have them printed.

Charles Le Brun, whose influence in these matters was considerable, opened this series of lectures in 1667, stating their purpose to be 'to give firm rules to those who wish to profess these noble arts'. At first the lectures were devoted to descriptions of pictures by Poussin, Raphael and Titian. But before long the academicians, having acquired some skill in the play of ideas, passed from the consideration of individual works to more general problems.

Some of these problems, such as, for instance, that of the relationship between and the respective merits of drawing and colour, could lead to violent controversy. What is fascinating is that what would appear now to be an 'academic' issue had in fact direct political implications. The protagonists were aware of this. For the first time in history, it seems, an aesthetic debate, on the subject of the plastic arts or the Fine Arts, reflected opposing political conceptions. The fierce defenders of drawing were the partisans of absolutism and of reason. Those who advocated the merits of colour belonged more to the political opposition and were in favour of granting more importance to the emotions.

Drawing addressed itself to the mind, colour to the senses. Drawing was an intellectual act, colour a mere accident subject to variations in light. Le Brun, defending absolutism in the Academy against colour, went so far as to draw on Cartesian metaphysics: 'Real merit subsists by itself and borrows nothing from outside itself.'[2] But colour depends on drawing, 'since it is incapable of representing or portraying anything except through the articulation of drawing'. Louis Hourticq, drawing a parallel between Descartes and Le Brun, comments: 'This for Le Brun is the strongest argument, the one that cannot be refuted because it is the metaphysical argument from *perfection*, the one that Descartes used to prove the existence of God.'[3]

Le Brun's position did not go unchallenged. He found a mettlesome adversary in the person of Roger de Piles, ambassador, connoisseur, theorist of painting, and practising portraitist. Nevertheless, in order to avoid the reprisals of absolutism he had in 1673 to publish anonymously his *Dialogue sur le coloris*, a homage to Rubens and to colour written in opposition to Poussin, the paragon of the official line. For a quarter of a century – until Le Brun's death in 1690 and the weakening of Louis XIV's absolutism – de Piles remained on the defensive. Not admitted to the Academy during this period, he was triumphantly received in 1699.

Under Le Brun the Academy raised painting to a dignity it had never before enjoyed. De Piles proceeded to liberate it from the constraints entailed by this elevation, and thus to clear the ground for a new advance by the religion of Art. For if it is true that the Academy had sought to elaborate a doctrine of art, it nevertheless insisted, like the Counter-Reformation, that artists must concentrate above all upon the subject matter. But the prime characteristic of the new religion of Art was that form was made superior to content.

This is what happened at the end of the Renaissance in Italy. Now the same tendency was to go from strength to strength from the eighteenth century until our own day.

In contrast to Félibien, who judged paintings according to the hierarchy of genres, de Piles introduced a series of criteria that had almost nothing to do with the subject represented on the canvas. He sought to distil from amongst the multiplicity of particular tastes 'a general taste', susceptible of purity and corruption and which, without being identified with any specific national or individual taste, underlay them all and was their common standard. He judged the relative value of painting on the basis of criteria such as composition, drawing, colouring or expression. He devised for the benefit of connoisseurs a 'Balance of Painters' in which about fifty artists of 'established merit' were given marks out of twenty on the basis of each of these four criteria. Here are the marks he gave to the following painters:[4]

	Composition	Drawing	Colouring	Expression	Total
Dürer	8	10	10	8	36
da Vinci	15	16	4	14	49
Michelangelo	8	17	4	8	37
Titian	12	15	18	6	51
Rubens	18	13	17	17	65
Poussin	15	17	6	15	53
Rembrandt	15	6	17	12	50

Anticipating criticism of this system of assessment from his contemporaries as well as posterity, de Piles wrote: 'I have attempted this more for my own amusement than to bring others round to my way of thinking. Opinions in this matter vary too much for it to be possible to believe that one's own is the only right one.'[5] What is so important here is the fact that de Piles judged pictures without regard to any considerations of a political or religious nature.

This tendency to judge works of art outside their social situation and apart from problems of school and nationality gained strength in the first half of the eighteenth century, with men like the Abbé Du Bos, Père André and the Abbé Batteux who were no longer either practising artists or connoisseurs. They no longer discussed technical problems of painting and sculpture (with which they were unfamiliar) but reasoned in the abstract about art as they would about metaphysics.

From now onwards it was the men of letters who were to influence modes of thought and feeling in the world of the plastic arts. The theoreticians of art, of the beautiful or of aesthetics were to be, simultaneously, theoreticians for both painters and writers. Thus were the ambitions realized and efforts rewarded of the painters and sculptors who had struggled since the Renaissance to achieve equality with the *litterati*. The painters of the seventeenth century, in order to confirm their status as intellectuals in the face of the world, and to secure for painting the prerogatives already acquired by poetry, had annexed to their cause a famous line of Horace: *'ut pictura poesis'* (poetry is like painting).

They thus elevated a passing comparison into an assertion of equality between the two arts. The analogy was repeated so often that the men of letters were finally convinced. They proclaimed that poetry and painting were sisters and that to be a painter one had to be a poet. The Abbé Batteux went even further: 'The two arts have between them so great a uniformity that if one has treated them together all one need do is change the terms and substitute painting, drawing, colouring for poetry, story, versification.'[6]

And now when the theoreticians of art spoke of beauty –

the two arts being interchangeable – it was understood that this referred as much to beauty created by the painter as to that created by the writer, and even by extension to that created by artists in other fields. As the word Beautiful, with a capital 'B' enters the vocabulary of the arts there is a new ambition to soar into a sphere above the merely human in time and space. The writers who seek unique or universal Beauty are in the same state of mind as those who seek to define God. And so we have the supreme irony of Diderot, one of the leading anti-religious writers of the eighteenth century, writing the article on the Beautiful for the *Encyclopédie* and choosing it as a specimen for separate printing, as a thirteenth-century encyclopaedist would no doubt have chosen the article on God. In his struggle against the established religion Diderot was unwittingly participating in the birth of another, the religion of Art.

The role of Frenchmen in the elaboration of this religion came to a momentary conclusion with Diderot. The initiative passed to Germany. In 1750 Baumgarten published his *Aesthetica*, which can be considered as the birth certificate of aesthetics as a discipline in its own right. There followed a whole crop of aesthetic systems elaborated by philosophers: Sulzer (1751), Lessing (1756), Mendelssohn (1757), Kant (1781), Fichte (1792), Schelling (1792), Hegel (1807). The summit had been reached: henceforth to think about art was to philosophize.

9 □ Art for art's sake

The theories of the German philosophers exercised a profound influence in nineteenth-century France on the development of the idea of art and on the conduct of artists through the intermediary of the literary movement of 'art for art's sake' (*l'art pour l'art*). German Romanticism of the end of the eighteenth century and French Romanticism of the beginning of the nineteenth brought about the re-emergence of the Renaissance artist, an exceptional and semi-divine being. The religion of Art achieved its final form, and artists the personality they have today.

It was under the influence of economic and political factors that the Germans became romantics and mystics. The mysticism of the German intelligentsia may have provided fertile ground for many generations of students of philosophy in Germany and other Western countries, but it also contributed to the misfortune of humanity by blunting the critical and rational spirit of German intellectuals in the face of another form of mysticism, that of Hitler.

The peculiar misfortune of Germany was not to have assimilated the Enlightenment of the eighteenth century and to have passed almost without transition from the Middle Ages to the modern period. Except for isolated individuals, rationalism did not penetrate German society. While in France the bourgeoisie had been rising slowly and steadily for two centuries, establishing itself in the higher echelons of administration in the seventeenth century and achieving intellectual preponderance, the German bourgeoisie already found its progress blocked in the sixteenth century. The prosperity of German cities was hit by the shift of international trade from the Mediterranean to the Atlantic. The bourgeoisie lost its economic power and, as a consequence, its cultural bearings. The Thirty Years' War brought about the ruin of German trade. The princes took advantage of the situation to reserve important appointments at their courts for noblemen and to confine the bourgeoisie to subordinate posts.

Exclusion from political activity bred a sense of frustration. Unable to make his mark in everyday reality, the bourgeois took refuge in an unreal world, in dreams, in the mysterious, the fantastic and the bizarre, in the past or in Utopia. He lost contact with the world and with the present. He felt lonely and isolated. He practised introspection and discovered the unconscious. And so in this milieu there emerged a new type of intellectual – the romantic.

The romantic was at odds with the world, an introvert who exalted emotion and rejected reason, who found in art, aesthetics or in beauty a compensation for his frustration. For the romantic, art was a surrogate, a consolation and a refuge. Art insulated him from the realism of the world at large. The romantic drew a line of demarcation between his private and his public existence, between art, which was an integral part of his moral life, and political life.

Under the impact of political upheaval the French intelligentsia of the early nineteenth century also became romantic. The post-revolutionary period was one of disillusionment. Writers were held responsible for the Revolution and lost the prestige they had enjoyed during the Enlightenment. No longer able to leave their mark on the course of history, they proceeded to isolate themselves from society as German intellectuals had done a few decades earlier. They condemned all political activity. Alfred de Musset exclaimed: 'Politics, alas! that is our misery. My best enemies advise me to engage in it, to be red in the evening, white the following day. Rather not, if I am read, I want to be re-read.'[1] And he derided humanitarians of all kinds, and men of action.

Alfred de Vigny declared with satisfaction that 'there will always be antipathy between the man of Power and the man of Art'.[2] He recommended 'the separation of poetic life from political life'.[3] And one of the ways he suggested to the poet to achieve this state of affairs was to 'employ all the forces of one's will to look away from the all too easy undertakings of the active life'.[4]

To avoid the active life despised by Vigny, the romantic retreated to an ivory tower. From there he anathematized all the forces hostile to his ideal: the academies and the churches for their traditionalism and authoritarianism, science for its utilitarianism, the bourgeoisie for its realism, its relentless pursuit of gain and its hypocrisy. The antithesis of the authorities, the scholar, and the bourgeois, each and all worthy of contempt, was for the romantic the artist, disinterested, free of care, full of nobility. He places him at the summit of the social hierarchy. He made of him an ideal being, a demigod. 'The artist,' wrote Victor Cousin, who was professor at the Sorbonne in the years preceding the Revolution of 1830, 'is animated by the feeling of beauty ... a pure and disinterested feeling', distinct 'from moral feeling and religious feeling'. Cousin proclaimed the autonomy of art: 'Art is referable to nothing but itself.'[5] He borrowed some of his ideas, notably that of the autonomy of art with regard to ethics and science, from the German idealist philosophers: Kant, Schiller, Schelling and Hegel. He met Hegel in Germany in 1842 and corresponded with him. The German aesthetic theories introduced in France by Cousin expressed in philosophical language what French romantics were confusedly groping towards.

The poet and novelist Théophile Gautier took up and developed these romantic theories in the preface to his book *Mademoiselle de Maupin* (1834). This preface, which contains a violent attack on the encroachments of bourgeois utilitarianism among intellectuals, is a manifesto for pure art. The following year a literary critic, Fortoul, attempting to define the ideas expressed in this manifesto, coined the phrase that was to have a long career: *'l'art pour l'art'*. In this preface Gautier to some extent systematized the thought of Romanticism at a time (1830–40) when some of the major romantic writers, such as Victor Hugo, Lamartine, and George Sand, were moving towards social or political art, while others, like

Musset and Vigny, took no sides or remained silent. On the other hand, the theories of 'art for art's sake' were taken up with enthusiasm by a new generation of neo-romantic writers: Flaubert, Baudelaire, Théodore de Banville, and the brothers Goncourt.

This new generation, disappointed by the attitude of those romantic poets who were compromised by the hostages they had given either to the bourgeoisie or to socialism, moved closer to the painters, who seemed to be keeping better faith with the ideals of form and beauty, chief among them Ingres and Delacroix, who dominated the history of French painting for over half a century, and who, each in his own way, became fervent disciples of art for art's sake. And it is in fact in painting and sculpture in the twentieth century that the doctrine of art for art's sake has achieved its perfect expression.

For Théophile Gautier art was not a means but an end, an end in itself. In the celebrated preface to *Mademoiselle de Maupin* he wrote:

What is really beautiful can be no other than good for nothing; anything that is useful is ugly because it expresses some need, and those of man are base and disgusting, like his wretched and invalid nature. The most useful part of a house is its latrines ... I am one of those to whom the superfluous is necessary, and I like things and people in inverse proportion to the services they render.[6]

Twenty years later he wrote in an article:

We believe in the autonomy of art ... an artist ceases to be one in our eyes when he pursues anything except the beautiful; we have never been able to understand the separation of form from idea ... a beautiful form is a beautiful idea, for what would a form be that expressed nothing. ... Art is not a product of society ... Art has nothing to do with ethics.[7]

To those who would have the poet take sides in the political conflicts of the day and who spoke to him of revolutions to come, Gautier replied that he was neither 'red nor white nor even tricolour', and did not notice revolutions except when windows were smashed by bullets.[8] 'I would gladly abdicate my rights as a Frenchman and a citizen to see an authentic picture by Raphael or a beautiful woman in the nude.'[9] Poetry need be neither morally edifying nor socially useful; in fact it serves no purpose outside itself.[10]

The adepts of this religion of Art lived like monks. 'They practised real asceticism,' writes Albert Cassagne in his *Théorie de l'art pour l'art en France*, 'by solitude and silence which leave the senses inactive and remove all causes of distraction to the mind, by banishing natural affections, they achieved not the actual fixation of ecstasy but the extreme concentration they needed in order to create.'[11] And, like monks, they rejected earthly love. Gautier admired Flaubert for his 'wisdom in not encumbering himself with wives, whether legitimate or illegitimate'.[12] He was convinced that had he opened his heart to a woman she would sooner or later have killed the feeling for art in him. The brothers Goncourt developed in two of their novels the theme of the destruction of the artist by a woman.

The devotees of art for art's sake lived in a state of aesthetic mysticism. 'The cult of an ideal above nature and above life, which others placed in religion, they placed in art; or rather art was for them a religion and, conversely, religion, in which by and large they did not believe, was a form of art, a popular form and hence inferior.'[13] 'Let us love each other in art as the mystics love each other in God,' exclaims Flaubert, 'and let everything else pale before this great love.'[14] And he confessed: 'I am turning to a kind of aesthetic mysticism .'[15] Théodore de Banville owned that he was one of those for whom art had always been an 'intolerant and jealous religion'.[16]

Among the painters, Ingres, whom Théophile Gautier celebrated as an 'Unconquered master, fervent priest of the beautiful who has preserved the mould of pure form',[17] proclaimed: 'Be religious about your art. ... Art is not merely a profession, it is an apostolate. ... My elevated tastes are part of a religion.'[18] Ingres, who is considered a classical painter, was in fact a romantic. He took himself for a demi-god, and his contemporaries, like the critic Théophile Silvestre, were aware of this: 'I can still hear his apostolic fulminations. For him art is a priesthood. Being infallible he does not engage in debate. A great man lives like a simple mortal. M. Ingres behaves like the pope, the vicar of God.'[19]

For Ingres what counted above all was form. For him, subjects from antiquity were not more than motifs. His passion for the beautiful made him, together with other disciples of art for art's sake, indifferent to the fortunes of his fellowmen. During the June revolution of 1848 he calmly finished his *Venus Anadyomène*. He despised the 'ignorant masses' and the times he lived in.

Delacroix, who is always contrasted with Ingres, was in fact very much like him. He professed the same cult of the beautiful – he had attended Cousin's lectures – the same passion for the 'motif', the same contempt for the masses and the times. Maxime Ducamp wrote of him: 'Like certain men of letters who have created art for art's sake, M. Delacroix had invented colour for colour's sake. Humanity and history have been for him but a motif for matching well-chosen nuances.'[20] Delacroix confirmed this: 'All subjects become worthy through the author's merit. O young artist, are you waiting for a subject? Everything is a subject, the subject is yourself, your impressions, your emotions in front of nature. You must look into yourself, not outside yourself.'[21]

Once a painter has declared that 'all subjects become worthy through the author's merit', and that the 'principal object of a picture is to be a feast for the eye', then it can be said that the only difference between a Madonna and a cabbage is an aesthetic one. Declarations of this kind annihilated the hierarchy of genres that had been established by the Academy in the seventeenth century. In asserting that the subject of painting is the painter himself, Delacroix defined modern painting. Before Romanticism, the artist had expressed more or less deliberately the feelings or the ideology of a social class; henceforth his aim would be to express no more than his own impressions and emotions. People would paint for their own personal satisfaction. Painting would cease to be a profession and would become a vocation.

It is not surprising to find painters from now on increasingly, if not misunderstood, at least unrecognized. Delacroix is a case in point. For a long time he was rejected and derided. 'M. Delacroix paints with a drunken broom,' wrote one art critic. People laughed in front of his pictures. 'For thirty years now I have been exposed to idiots'[22] was his comment. In the Salon of 1822 his *Dante and Virgil* provoked clamorous hostility, and in 1827 the jury rejected his *Death of Sardanapalus*. It was only at the auction after his death that his pictures fetched high prices.

Delacroix sought escape from the contemporary world by painting historical and oriental scenes, as Ingres did by painting mythological ones. Corot escaped from the life around him by painting landscapes and ruins devoid of any political or social significance. When he paints the Forum in Rome he is not meditating on the ruins, he is thinking about the colour of the burnt stones and the brilliance of the sky. Corot was a thorough-going adept of art for art's sake. 'What I look for,' he wrote, 'is form, the whole, the tone values.'[23] The subject did not interest him. 'I paint a woman's breast as I would paint an ordinary milk can.'[24] Corot sold his first picture at the age of fifty years, nine months and twenty-one days.

Nowadays the French bourgeoisie are reproached for buying scarcely any work by the Delacroixs, the Corots, the Manets, the Cézannes and the Van Goghs during their own lifetime and for allowing some of these artists to languish in the most desperate of material difficulties. The bourgeois is called a Philistine. But this is surely unfair to him, considering that even among French intellectuals only a minority defended the doctrine of art for art's sake. Even the most celebrated French art critic of the nineteenth century, the champion of pure Beauty, Charles Baudelaire, shamefully foreswore what he had once adored under the pressure of events in 1848. He wrote on that occasion: 'The puerile utopia of art for art's sake, by excluding morality and sometimes even passion, was necessarily sterile. ... In the name of the superior principles which govern universal life, we are entitled to declare it guilty

of heterodoxy.'[25] In such a situation, cannot the poor bourgeois plead attentuating circumstances?

In order to understand the attitude of the bourgeois and his
suspicion of all new painting, one must take account of a
factor that weighed heavy in his judgements: the aggressive
and often ridiculous attitude towards him manifested by some
of the bohemian artists. Romanticism encouraged artists to
scandalize the bourgeois and play tricks on him. As a result
the latter could no longer tell whether an artist was being
sincere or not. He began to distrust artistic productions in so
far as they differed from those of the past. There are still traces
of this attitude today.

For the nineteenth-century bourgeois, artists were
bohemians with long hair and beards, who dressed eccen-
trically and led a desultory, carefree and promiscuous existence. To a certain extent the public still thinks of artists in this
way. It is a literary, idealized image created by Henri Murger
in his *Scènes de la vie bohème* (1847). In fact, this kind of
existence was lived only by a rather insignificant group of
fanatical supporters of art for art's sake. Certainly it had
nothing in common with the lives of a Delacroix or a
Flaubert.

Bohemianism first appeared about 1830 represented by a
group of happy-go-lucky young men in the orbit of Théophile
Gautier, constantly on the lookout for good tricks to be
played on the bourgeois Philistines, neither rich nor poor,
subsidized by their partners and, eventually, making their way
in life. The second generation of bohemians, those that
Murger knew, were both poorer and less talented, impreg-
nated with the doctrine of art for art's sake and Alfred de
Vigny's theories on the fate of the poet. Vigny's *Stello*, published in 1831, and his *Chatterton*, first performed in 1835,
disseminated the myth that the poet and the artist are always
misunderstood by the society they live in, the myth that they
are martyrs to society, doomed to die of hunger.

10 □ Social art in the service of freedom

In 1865 there appeared a posthumous work by Proudhon, socialist and revolutionary: *Du principe de l'art et de sa destination sociale*. The disciples of *l'art pour l'art* were outraged. Flaubert wrote: 'We now have the maximum of socialist caddishness.'[1] The work, today almost forgotten, should be read by all those interested in the origins of socialist realism and, more generally, in the relationship between art and society, a problem almost completely ignored by Marx.

In this book Proudhon attacks Romanticism as a morality for outlaws which had been 'the most powerful of all the agents of our intellectual dissolution'.[2] As for art for art's sake, being based on nothing, it is nothing. He inveighs against the emptiness of Ingres and reproaches Delacroix for treating his subjects according to his 'personal impressions'. Both arrive at the same result, which is irrationality. Their works reflect their contempt for the world around them. They do not believe in progress. Proudhon regrets that in his struggle for the moral and social improvement of mankind he cannot count on them. He considers that artists have a part to play in the realization of a new world. In opposition to art for art's sake he proposes the notion of social art.

The idea goes back to Diderot. Jacques Louis David – to whom Diderot transferred his support after his disappointment with Greuze – had taken it up and in the year 2 of the Republic, prescribed an educative and moral purpose for painting and sculpture. At the beginning of the nineteenth century this conception of the role of art in society reappears in the Utopia of Saint-Simon.

In the ideal society which he imagined, Saint-Simon

accorded the highest place to those he called 'producers' – scientists and manufacturers. The idle were condemned. At the nation's head, beside the scientists and manufacturers, he installed the artists. These had a socially useful role to play. It would be their task to propagate Saint-Simonian ideas and thus help to bring about changes in institutions, social customs and beliefs. They would declare the excellence of work, industry and science; help in the emancipation of women and the enfranchisement of the working class; cultivate sentiments conducive to the development of humanity. For Saint-Simon and his disciples, artists were in fact destined to become leaders of men. They were to be invested with a kind of sacerdotal power and act as priests, spiritual directors, magi; to be the preceptors of mankind and the prophets of progress. Instead of following society they were to march at the head of it, to be the spearhead of civilization.

Saint-Simon proclaimed the dignity of the artist who works in the interest of the community. For the romantic enamoured of what is dead, turned towards the past, dwelling on his own emotions, egoist and egocentric, he had no use. The liberal Catholics, with Lamennais at their head, and the republicans shared this view of the romantic. Both groups found shocking the amorality of romantic art, its uselessness to the people, its catering for the amusement of the idle. Like the Saint-Simonians, Lamennais thought of the social role of the artist as that of a prophet. 'Art for art's sake is therefore an absurdity.'[3] He considered that artists 'by descending into the bowels of society can capture the pulse of life beating there and impart it to their work, which it will animate as the Spirit of God animates and fills the universe'.[4] Art must regenerate society.

As for the republicans, they did not conceal their hope of harnessing art and the products of the imagination to their social idea. Armand Mansart wrote from prison in 1834: 'Art and labour are the elements of republican opinion, they are the two forces with which it will sooner or later take possession of the world.'[5] Art must address itself to the people in order to raise their moral standards and initiate them into republican principles.

The appeals made to the artists and poets by the Saint-Simonians, the liberal Christians and the republicans to forsake their ivory tower were heeded by some of the leading romantics: Victor Hugo, Lamartine, George Sand. They were flattered to be seen in the role of providential beings and to be called upon to initiate the masses.

Hugo, a declared champion of the independence of the poet and opponent of the 'puerile theory' of utilitarian art, evolved towards social art under the combined impact of Saint-Simonianism and the events of 1830. He discovered the artist to have a sacred mission and exalted his civilizing and moral role. In 1840 he wrote: 'The poet, living in impious days, seeks to prepare for better days. ... Resembling the prophets, he lights up the future and in every age brandishes it like a torch over the heads of all.'[6] Poets were the shepherds of nations.

Lamartine's evolution was similar to that of Hugo. In 1825 he had written: 'Loving, praying, singing – that is my life.' But by 1832: 'Shame on him who can sing while Rome is burning if he has not the soul, the lyre and the eyes of Nero!'[7] Once converted to social ideas, Lamartine devoted a great deal of his energy to political writing and action; and he, the celebrated romantic poet, wrote to one of his friends: 'Poetry should be no more than a distraction of our leisure hours, an ornament of life.'[8]

Against a chorus of protests from the devotees of art for art's sake, George Sand together with the socialist Pierre Leroux, founded in 1841 the *Revue independante*, for which she wrote *Consuelo* and which became the principal organ of the supporters of social art. It printed verse by worker poets and tried to attract towards socialism the great names in poetry and fiction. In 1848 George Sand greeted with enthusiasm the proclamation of the Republic, drafted circulars to town mayors, and wrote some of the *Bulletins de la République* as well as numerous articles in support of the popular cause.

Some artists, like Daumier and Courbet, also supported social art and joined in the struggle for political freedom. For this one of them went to prison and the other into exile. For such artists, the evolution of the political regimes and the revolutions of 1830, 1848 and 1871 affected the course of their lives considerably.

In 1830 the Republicans, disappointed by the July revolution in which they had taken a major part, and debarred from power by Louis-Philippe and the bourgeoisie, appealed to republican artists to fight against the government. Taking advantage of the freedom of the Press granted under the new charter, Charles Philipon, an ardent republican and polemicist, founded *La Caricature* and gathered round him collaborators like Daumier, Granville and Traviès. The ferocious political cartoons they began to turn out made the whole of France laugh and were far more dangerous to the new regime than vehement articles and fiery speeches, the plottings of secret societies or workers' riots. Art, having only too often been a weapon of propaganda or prestige in the hands of the ruling classes, this time became a weapon in the fight for the people and for liberty.

But the bourgeois government could not tolerate the caricaturists' assaults on its authority for long. Legal proceedings were taken out in order to scotch Philipon and his team; on 19 November 1831 he was sentenced to six months' imprisonment for having represented the King in the form of a pear. The following year Daumier was interned at Sainte-Pélagie for his famous caricature of Louis-Philippe as Gargantua, devouring France's wealth and passing it on to the French peerage. Here Daumier was expressing the resentment of the working classes against the profiteers of the July monarchy. On his release he continued to attack the government. In 1834 he engraved an epic scene, the rue Transnonain massacre in Lyons, where troops in a riot shot down an innocent worker family. The engraving was seized.

On 9 September 1835 the government, fearing for its existence, promulgated a shameful law suppressing the freedom of the Press and prohibiting political caricature. This form of social art, which had caused the regime to tremble, thus found itself muzzled. Until 1848 Daumier had to content himself with satirizing the bourgeois way of life. The revolution of February 1848, which saw the fall of Louis-Philippe and the proclamation of the Second Republic, allowed Daumier to take up his pencil once more as a political satirist.

The period between the February revolution and the *coup d'état* by Louis Napoléon on 2 December saw a flowering of social art. Many writers and artists who under the July monarchy had been supporters of art for art's sake, either from conviction or under the pressure of events, now abandoned it and threw themselves openly into the social and political struggle. The re-establishment of censorship after the *coup d'état* of 2 December 1851 and the increased powers of the police under the new imperial regime drove many writers and artists back to art for art's sake. Daumier was silenced again. He re-emerged, an old man, after 1870. Imbued with liberal and humanitarian ideas, he died in near-destitution.

A number of artists little known or not greatly esteemed today, like Gleyre, Thomas Couture, Jules Breton, Jeanron and Bonhommé, defended Saint-Simonian or socialist ideas after 1830. Gleyre designed a large triptych, *The Past, the Present and the Future,* while Thomas Couture exhibited at the Salon his *Love of Gold,* Jules Breton his *Hunger,* Jeanron his *Charity of the People or the Blacksmiths of Corrèze* and Bonhommé his *Miners of Fourchambault.* Louis Hautecoeur says in his *Littérature et peinture en France du XVIIe au XXe siècle* that what these pictures represented was a 'new class attempting to conquer a place in society, as the bourgeoisie had done in the eighteenth and at the beginning of the nineteenth century'.[9] These painters drew attention for the first time not to 'popular characters but to the people',[10] no longer to the picturesque workman but to the working class.

Millet, who never made any secret of his republican opinions and his sympathy with the poor, painted peasants at work. At the Salon of 1849 his *Sower, Sewing Women* and *Sheaf-Binders* were pronounced to be of a 'proletarian' inspiration. In 1857 *Le Figaro* and *La Presse,* reviewing the *Gleaners,* called him a demagogue. Delacroix, whose anti-democratic feelings break out constantly in his *Journal* – he was against the freedom of the Press and social or technical progress of any kind – attacked Millet as one of the 'pleiad or gang of artists who took part in the revolution of 1848, or approved of it, believing apparently that there would be equality both of talent and of wealth'.[11] Millet made no distinction between great subjects and small subjects. 'Why should the action of planting potatoes or beans be less interesting or less noble than any other action … ? It is the human, the purely human aspect that moves me most in art.'[12] After his death his famous *Angelus* was bought for 800,000 francs and the *Shepherdess* for the fabulous sum of 1,200,000 (over 3,000,000 in present-day currency). The socialist realism of the period paid a handsome dividend.

The most celebrated representative of this nineteenth-century socialist realism was without doubt Gustave Courbet. At this time socialist realism was in opposition. The Saint-Simonians found in him a painter who adopted with enthusiasm their theories about the exalted station of the artist and his moral role in society. Courbet portrayed everyday life without prettification. He did not idealize his characters, and thus affronted the bourgeois who did not want to see the poverty and misery that surrounded him: 'Realism is a savage type of painting in which art is degraded and debased.' At the Salon of 1853 Napoleon III struck with his crop across the buttocks of Courbet's *Bathers* and called them 'draught mares'. Some of Courbet's paintings were protests against the clerical, bourgeois and authoritarian regime of the Second Empire. He attempted vast canvasses with a moral message. In the *Artist's Studio* he placed on one side the exploited – the poacher, the harvester, the worker and the prostitute – and on the other the exploiters. In the *Return from the Conference* he attacked parish priests who were active supporters of the imperial regime. He showed them drunk. The imperial police intervened and stopped the picture being exhibited.

In his struggle to reform society, Proudhon took up Courbet. What he found in Courbet – as Diderot had in Greuze – was a painter capable of translating a progressive morality into images. Proudhon commented approvingly on

Courbet's work – again as Diderot had done on Greuze's –
and not infrequently over-interpreted it; and made Courbet
say things he had never imagined.[13] But Courbet came to
believe that his paintings did express what the philosopher
saw in them, and he attributed to some of his works, such as
The Stone Breakers, a social import that was probably not
part of their original conception.

In the eyes of the bourgeoisie, Courbet was a dangerous
socialist activist. His somewhat vehement declarations of
principle did nothing to dispel this notion. The fact that he
rallied to the Commune in 1871 seemed to confirm it. Once
the rising had been suppressed, the bourgeoisie had their
revenge for Courbet's aggressive attacks on them. He was
arrested on 7 June 1871 and interned at Sainte-Pélagie. He
was charged before a court martial in Versailles with having
been the prime mover in the demolition of the Colonne
Vendôme, a symbol of Bonapartist militarism. The charge
was unfounded. As documentary evidence shows, all he did
was to suggest in the months that preceded the demolition
that the reliefs decorating the column should be deposited at
Les Invalides. Nevertheless he was sentenced to six months'
imprisonment and, on release, had to leave the country, as the
government claimed from him the entire cost of the recon-
struction of the column. He died in Switzerland in 1877 in
considerable poverty, in some ways a martyr of Saint-
Simonianism.

The effect of this trial was to confirm the French bourgeoisie for generations to come in their belief that some artists
– whom they had already learned to distrust at the time of
Romanticism – were a potential source of danger to the
bourgeois social order.

Courbet was the last painter of note to be associated with
social art. After him Saint-Simonian doctrines about the social
and moral role of the artist went out of fashion. Under the
combined influence of aesthetic theories and photography,
which we shall deal with in the following chapter, artists
moved again towards art for art's sake. Nevertheless the
passionate rhetoric of Saint-Simonians proclaiming to the

world that artists are in the vanguard of civilization is always listened to with pride and joy by artists of all tendencies. Such declarations, combined with the often similar ones made by the romantics and the devotees of art for art's sake, have convinced the artists that they are predestined to be men who stand above the common ruck of humanity.

11 □ 1839

On Monday, 19 August 1839, François Arago informed the Académie des Sciences and the Académie des Beaux-Arts, meeting in joint session at the Institut Français, that two Frenchmen, Niepce and Daguerre, had succeeded in fixing chemically the images formed inside the *camera obscura*, used by many painters for several centuries. Photography the thing, though not yet the word, had been officially born. It is difficult for us to imagine today the excitement with which the announcement was greeted, amongst scientists and artists and by the general public. How wonderful to be able to obtain an image of nature without the intervention of an artist! The artist's hand had been replaced by light! People at once began to speak of the 'pencil of nature' and of 'drawing by light'. But what troubled the artists was that the image obtained in this way revealed things that the artist's eye had never observed. 'Shadows and lights', wrote Delacroix, 'are reproduced in it in their true character.'[1]

The artists reacted – although in different ways – to this discovery which affected them all so closely. On the way out of the famous meeting at the Institut, the painter Delaroche is said to have declared: 'Painting is dead.' Some time later Ingres is supposed to have exclaimed: 'Which of us would be capable of such fidelity, of such firmness in the interpretation of lines, of such delicacy in the modelling ... ? Photography is a very beautiful thing ... very beautiful but one must not admit it.'[2] Some artists attempted to 'correct the errors of the eye'[3] in their own paintings – to paint photographically. Others deliberately moved away from realism. It is the latter who were to be regarded by posterity as the great masters of modern art. The former were to lapse into almost total oblivion. 1839 is a watershed in the history of Western painting.

Until the invention of photography, from the Renaissance onwards in particular, it had been the ambition of most painters, whether they were portrait painters, historical painters or landscape painters, to reproduce reality as closely as possible. 'The most excellent painting,' wrote Leonardo da Vinci, 'is that which imitates nature best and produces pictures which conform most closely to the object portrayed.'[4] To achieve this artists had recourse, from the fifteenth century onwards, to various optical devices. At the beginning of the sixteenth century Dürer describes four different types of mechanical aids for drawing in perspective in order to reproduce reality very exactly. Leonardo himself, describing one of the optical processes that enable the artist to draw a landscape with precision, explains the principle of the *camera obscura*:

When the images of illuminated objects pass through a small hole into a very dark room, if you receive them on a piece of white paper placed vertically in the room at some distance from the aperture, you will see on the paper all these objects in their natural shapes and colours. ... If these images come from a place which is illuminated by the sun, they will seem as if painted on the paper which must be very thin, and must be viewed from behind.[5]

The phenomenon of the *camera obscura* was known to Aristotle, and was regularly used by Arab and medieval scholars, particularly in order to study eclipses. Leonardo is the first artist to mention the principle, and in 1558 the Neapolitan Giovanni Battista Porta suggested its use for drawing and painting. Thirty years later he introduced an improvement, a convex lens fitted into the hole, which gave a clearer image. At the beginning of the seventeenth century a portable *camera obscura* was devised, a box with a convex lens in one side and a translucent screen opposite for receiving the image. This was the ancestor of the modern camera.

It is now thought likely that Jan Vermeer, a painter whom the world of art considers as one of the greatest geniuses in the history of Western painting (an artist whose works, if they came on the market, would probably fetch prices higher than the record sum of £820,000 paid for Rembrandt's *Aristotle contemplating the Bust of Homer*), used the *camera obscura* for some of his paintings. His *View of Delft*, with its wide angle of vision, its extraordinary detail of stones and leaves, its figures which are as though integrated into the setting, is curiously reminiscent of the panoramic views that one is invited to admire in the modern versions of the *camera obscura* installed in some tourist centres. If Vermeer did use the *camera obscura*, the lenses for it may well have been made by the great naturalist Leewenhoek, who lived in Delft and was appointed 'curator' of Vermeer's estate after the painter's death.

There were probably other Dutch painters who made use of the aid of a clear image on a translucent screen. In the following century Reynolds, who used the *camera obscura* for his portraits, writes with appreciation about the paintings (among others, Vermeer's *Milkmaid*) he saw on a visit to Holland: 'Dutch pictures are a representation of nature, just as it is seen in a *camera obscura*.'[6] In the course of the eighteenth century the use of the device became widespread. Algarotti wrote in 1762: 'The best modern painters [of vedute] among the Italians have availed themselves greatly of this contrivance; nor is it possible they should have otherwise represented things so much to the life.'[7] Contemporary engravings show artists in the country with their *camera obscura*, which had become as much part of their equipment as the easel.

'Likenesses' were much sought after at the time and this brought in its train the invention of a number of mechanical devices for producing portraits cheaply. In the second half of the century silhouette portraits in profile, made by tracing the shadow cast by the sitter's face, enjoyed a great vogue. In 1786 Chrétien, a Versailles musician, devised the *physionotrace*, an apparatus for tracing, with a high degree of precision, three-quarter life-size portraits. These were reduced on to copper plates from which a dozen or more copies could then be run off as required. In 1807 William Wollaston introduced what he called the *camera lucida,* an instrument consisting of a prism which projects on to a sheet of paper a precise image of the face to be drawn.

For some artists the representation of reality was not enough. They wanted to create the illusion of reality. In 1787 an Irish painter, Robert Barker, registered a patent for a 'panorama' (panoramic painting based on the same principle as the circarama today). The spectator, placed in semi-obscurity in the centre of a circle formed by a painting over a hundred metres long and sixteen metres tall depicting every-day or historical scenes, had the illusion of being in the midst of the events depicted. In Paris Napoleon I had his victories painted in this way. In his diorama, set up in 1822, Daguerre painted vast pictures on transparent surfaces combined with a system of changing light effects, which took the illusion of reality a stage further. Music or appropriate sounds accom-panied the spectacle. In the *Midnight Mass at St Etienne-du-Mont* the church is first seen in daylight, then darkness falls and candles are lit. The congregation arrive and take their places. Midnight mass is celebrated. The spectacle ends with the break of dawn.

To enhance yet further the dramatic effect of these pictures, which he painted with the aid of a *camera obscura,* Daguerre tried to produce luminous pigments. He experimented with chemical substances sensitive to light. This launched him in pursuit of a dream common to other investigators in the field: to fix chemically the images formed in the *camera obscura.* He heard that Nicéphore Niepce, a practical scientist living in Chalon-sur-Saône, had solved the problem but that his method could not be commercialized. A skilful businessman, Daguerre entered into a partnership with Niepce, who died in 1833. Daguerre improved Niepce's method and gave it his own name: the 'daguerreotype'. Thus it was that on 19 August 1839 artists learned with stupefaction that they were confronted by a potential rival.

They were to be haunted by this rival up to the end of the century and beyond. It was no longer possible for a painter to apply his brush to canvas without being aware, consciously or unconsciously, of the photographic image. Conversely, photographers would try to model themselves on painters. The give and take between the two media became very complex, especially the influence of photography on painting which has until recently received little attention in books on art history. In 1963 André Vigneau brought the problem into focus in his *Brève histoire de l'art de Niepce à nos jours*.

In the midst of such a succession of events, of so many innovations that radically modified the foundations of a long-established aesthetic, the most important event is Cézanne, or rather Niepce-Cézanne. The hyphen is quite deliberate. I do believe that without Niepce, without Niepce's invention, Cézanne would not have been the Cézanne that 'revealed' himself the way he did.[8]

Painters and photographers remained generally on good terms with each other until 1859. It could hardly have been otherwise, for many painters – Delacroix, Horace Vernet, Degas – practised photography, while a number of photographers – David Hill, Charles Nègre, Nadar – had begun as painters and continued to paint occasionally.

At the first public exhibition of photographs in 1839, held in rue des Jeûneurs in Paris, the 'photogenized drawings' of Hyppolyte Bayard were hung among painters' canvasses. Paintings were judged in terms of photography and vice versa. At the time it was widely thought that the two skills might eventually merge into one. Links were established in view of this marriage, such as photo-painting and *cliché-verre*. Photo-painting consisted in 'projecting an enlargement of the negative of a portrait from the plate on to sensitized canvas so as to obtain a life-size print. ... All that remains to be done is to add to this photographic enlargement the colours of the original with a brush.'[9] The *cliché-verre*, on the other hand, consisted in etching a drawing on a glass plate coated with collodion, which could then be copied on photographic paper. Corot found this method very attractive.

In the years following the announcement of the discovery of the daguerreotype process, it was sometimes difficult to distinguish between a hand-coloured daguerreotype and a miniature, for the idea was soon hit upon of colouring by hand what the sun recorded in black and white. Miniature painters were employed to perform this delicate work. In bourgeois drawing-rooms miniatures and painted daguerreotypes could be seen hanging side by side in similar frames.

For painters the photographic camera was an improvement on the *camera obscura*. Images recorded in the open air could be brought back to the studio and worked on at leisure. Delacroix photographed models in specified poses which he could then study and draw from. He, and many other painters, also used albums of photographs especially compiled for the purpose.

When the conflict between painters and photographers broke out, Delacroix was one of the few artists to side openly with the camera. 'Truly, if a man of genius uses the daguerreotype as it should be used, he will rise to unknown heights.'[10] He estimated dispassionately the advantages and limitations of the mechanical image: 'The daguerreotype is the mirror of the object. Certain details, almost always neglected in drawings from nature, take on a great importance and thus lead the artist to a complete knowledge of construction.' However: 'It should be borne in mind that the daguerreotype is to be considered only as a translator appointed to initiate us further into the secrets of nature, for, in spite of the extraordinary degree of reality it achieves in some parts, it is only a reflection of reality, a copy, which is, in a certain sense, false, thanks to its very exactness.'[11]

Continuing his discussion of the daguerreotype, Delacroix reveals to us one of the psychological causes of the conflict between painters and photographers: this was the inferiority complex which began to be felt by the painters whose policy was systematically to correct their paintings so that they resembled photographic images. 'They are crushed by the tantalizing perfection of certain effects they find on the photographic plate. The harder they try to emulate these the more aware they become of their weakness.'[12] Some of the fiercest opposition to photography was to come from those who practised 'photographic painting'.

Photographers, on the other hand, grew more confident as improvements were added to the image-fixing process and as they saw painters becoming more dependent on them. Théophile Gautier commented ironically on this dependence: 'The daguerreotype, which has not been mentioned, which has earned no medal, has yet done a great deal for the exhibition [Salon of 1861]; it has supplied much information, spared models a great many poses, recorded accessories, backgrounds and draperies which only needed to be copied and coloured.'[13]

Three years after Arago's communication to the Institut, the London *Spectator* advised painters what to do:

Not all the delicate truth of photographic delineation can supply the want of colour: by imitating the local colour and atmospheric effect alone can landscape painters hope to stand against such a formidable rival as Nature. Therefore it behoves them to study with redoubled assiduity the influence of atmospheric light upon the individual hues of objects and the general tone of the scene; and also to strive to imitate the appearance of movement in figures and foliages, water and clouds.[14]

The Impressionists, for their part, were to take the *Spectator*'s advice.

Gradually, photographers became aware of themselves as members of a profession. In 1851 the first Heliographic Society was founded in Paris, and in 1859 a photographic Salon was held next door to the Salon of the Academy into which the photographers hoped to be admitted. For them photography had become an art on a par with painting, sculpture and engraving. Were they not portraitists, landscapists, even – with the advent of the Crimean War – history painters? They claimed competence in all genres, even allegory. To prove this a Swede, Oskar G. Rejlander, composed a vast allegory in 1857, a veritable photo-montage involving thirty negatives of 78 x 41 cm. The work was shown in Manchester at a large exhibition of art treasures, and was bought by Queen Victoria. Other photographers explored similar possibilities. Their pressure to gain recognition for photography as one of the Fine Arts began to worry painters. In his review of the 1859 Salon – the Salon of the Academy, of course – Charles Baudelaire launched a violent and prejudiced counterattack in the name of art. Photography was not an art but an industry. 'Let it return to its true function which is to be the handmaiden of the Sciences and the Arts.'[15] This pronouncement by the Messiah of Art has been gospel to the French intelligentsia ever since. Photography has never recovered from its effects.

The *coup de grâce* came three years later, in 1863, when a group of twenty-six painters, including Ingres, Isabey and Puvis de Chavannes, signed a manifesto, the 'purpose of which was to protest officially and to ask the authorities of the State for protection':

> Considering that photography amounts to a series of entirely manual procedures which require, no doubt, a certain familiarity with the operations they involve but that the reproductions that are the result of these cannot in any circumstances be assimilated to works of art which are the fruit of intelligence and of the study of art – for these reasons the artists undersigned protest against any assimilation that might be made of photography to art.[16]

Eugène Delacroix did not sign the manifesto.

The joke is that painters were now abusing photographers in the very terms that were used against themselves before Ficino's time by men of the Liberal Arts: as manual and mechanical workers. Artists have short memories! Having themselves gained admission to the citadel of the arts – which in due course became the Fine Arts – painters and sculptors shut the door firmly behind them. It remained shut to photographers throughout the last century, as it has done to the cinema, radio and television in this. The Fine Arts today are 'established' to the point of sclerosis. They owe their survival to tradition, aesthetics and money.

The refusal of painters to recognize photography as one of the Fine Arts saddled the photographers with a distracting case to prove. Instead of concentrating on the intrinsic possibilities of the camera they attempted, with the help of effects of lighting, focus and retouching, to compete with painting on its own ground. Thus in the last decades of the century some photographers made themselves ridiculous by attempting to emulate Impressionism.

Baudelaire's counterattack and the manifesto of the twenty-six mark a turning point not only in the relations between painters and photographers but also in those of painters among themselves. They now divided into two distinct groups which began to drift further and further apart. On one side there were those who turned their back on photography, those whom posterity was to group together as Impressionists – Degas, Manet, Monet ... ; on the other, those who continued to make servile use of the camera – Horace Vernet, Detaille, Meissonier .... The former strove to make fun of those who were the slaves of the lens. Théophile Silvestre wrote of Horace Vernet that he was a 'daguerreotype that sees and reproduces everything without thinking'.[17] Not that the various Impressionist painters ignored photography. They did not remain indifferent to the constant technical advances such as the rendering of movement and the snapshot. They attempted to introduce these into their own work. But the photographic image was for them a stimulus, not a master.

Of all the painters Edgar Degas was probably the one who was most stimulated by photography. Paul Valéry, who knew him well, writes: 'He understood what photography could teach the painter and what the painter ought to avoid borrowing from it ... besides, he liked and appreciated photography at a time when artists spurned it and dared not admit that they were using it. He took fine photographs himself...'[18] Degas was in fact a keen amateur photographer. He 'composed' his pictures like paintings. In a letter to Ludovic Halévy he comments critically on one of these compositions, a parody of Ingres' *Apotheosis of Homer*, with which he is not satisfied: 'I should have grouped my three Muses and my two choir boys against a white or light background. The women's figures in particular have not come out. Also the people should have been put closer together.'

Renoir and Mallarmé sat for Degas. When he painted, he could not forget certain photographic procedures such as centring. In some of his pictures, legs or parts of bodies are cut off by the edge of the canvas as though he were a photographer standing too close to his subject. He painted from photographs in order to capture certain fugitive expressions registered in a brief exposure. Some years ago the sitter for the *Portrait of an Unknown Woman* at the Tate Gallery was identified as the Princess Metternich. She had been photographed with her husband, and Degas, attracted no doubt by the strange and charming expression caught in the photograph, had been content to paint the princess and simply omit the prince.

Degas introduced the snapshot effect into his painting under the influence of what was being achieved in photography. Until 1859 daguerreotypes had not been capable of registering movement to any significant extent, mainly owing to the length of the time of exposure, originally several minutes. The camera could not capture people passing in the streets, and sitters for portraits had to remain motionless for long periods of time. When it became possible to reduce posing time to a few fractions of a second, people were astonished to discover that the gestures and positions of figures in motion were in fact unknown. Degas tried to fix this unstable moment when a person is no longer posing, but simply living in front of the painter at work. The artist wanted to be as sensitive as the photographic plate. To accentuate this snapshot effect, Degas was careful not to elaborate his pictures, thus equating speed of vision with speed of execution. 'The camera,' writes Louis Hautecoeur, 'sees and records at once the whole and the details. Our eye sees the whole but takes time to enumerate all the details. Our hand takes yet more time to represent them. The artist will content himself with the general effect. The quick sketch will replace the carefully worked out and painted picture.'[19] Contemporary critics spoke of snapshots in connection with Degas' painting, and this exasperated him; he had no desire to recognize the influence of photographic technique on his work. 'The snapshot,' he said, 'is photography and nothing more.'

The nature of human gait as revealed by the snapshot caused astonishment. But this was nothing compared with the disturbance caused by Eadweard Muybridge's photographs of running horses taken in California. In 1878 Muybridge mounted twelve cameras along a racecourse. Threads were laid across the track attached to each camera, so that a horse running through broke them one after the other, thus triggering off a succession of exposures. The twelve pictures so obtained were projected in a zoopraxiscope (an ancestor of our cine-projector) which gave an animated synthesis of the analytical stills. The positions of the legs of the horse in motion revealed by the camera were so different from the traditional rendering by artists that some painters, like Meissonier, thought at first that the camera was wrong: 'He gave a cry of astonishment and accused our apparatus of false vision.'[20] In order to be sure that he was painting galloping horses correctly, Meissonnier proceeded to have a circular railway built in his park. He rode round in it drawing the horses, which were made to run level with the train. In 1881 he finally capitulated before the evidence – the camera had been right. He corrected all his racehorses 'photographically'. Degas had had more confidence in the camera: he had discreetly corrected the gait of his horses.

Muybridge's work was followed up in France by the famous physiologist Jules-Etienne Marey. The experiments of both men on human and animal locomotion were stages on the way to the invention, at the end of the century, of the cinematograph.

Jean Renoir in his book about his father records:

The Impressionists attached considerable importance to the latest developments in photography. Their friend Charles Cros saw in it a means of studying the problems of the analysis of light and, in consequence, of making further experiments with Impressionism. Seurat, whom my father knew only slightly, believed that movement could be studied through photography. He was very much interested in the 'photographic gun' invented by Marey. Renoir regarded photography as both a great good and a great evil, 'like all inventions since the world began'. He gave due credit to Niepce and Daguerre for having 'freed painting from the lot of tiresome chores, starting with family portraits. Now the good shopkeeper has only to go to the photographer round the corner. So much the worse for us, but so much the better for the art of painting.[21]

Edouard Manet was no doubt the first to 'liberate' painting in this way. In 1859, the year of Baudelaire's famous counterblast against photography, Manet, probably under Baudelaire's influence, painted a picture for the Salon which was refused – as many others would be in the future – *The Absinthe Drinker*. This work can be considered as one of the earliest deliberately non-photographic paintings. Manet has painted the man and the absinthe bottle with a double shadow, which is obviously contrary to the laws of optics. Four years later Manet exhibited a painting *Mlle V. as an Espada*, in which he ignores the most elementary rules of perspective. Manet's painting was beginning to show a tendency towards abstraction. A contemporary art critic, Gonzague Privat, noted in 1865 that it was probably the over-abstract aspect of Manet's painting that made it incomprehensible to the public.

Manet's painting is not only non-photographic; it is also, paradoxically, non-realist, even though we know that he frequently chose realist subjects. But Manet's subjects were no more than 'motifs', occasions for producing oppositions of tones. He often ran out of ideas and asked his friends for suggestions. He seldom attempted either psychological penetration or anecdote in his work. Historical exactness meant little to him. He painted the side wound in his *Dead Christ* on the wrong side. For him, the greatest insult was to be called a history painter.

Contrary to a belief widely held today, Manet and the other 'revolutionary' artists found quite a few contemporary art critics to understand and defend them vigorously. This rallying to their side is to be explained largely by the spread in the literary milieu of the cult of Beauty and of the theories of art for art's sake. By moving away from photographic reality, artists like Manet, Monet and Cézanne were entering the domain of aestheticism in pursuit of form and colour. It was quite natural for Baudelaire to find himself at Manet's side when the painter was attacked. And Emile Zola too; he flew to Manet's rescue in 1867 in defence of *Olympia*:

And tell them loud and clear, *cher maître*, that a picture is for you but a pretext for analysis. You needed a female nude and you chose Olympia, the first woman you came across; you needed light spots and you placed in a corner a negress and a cat. What does all this mean? You do not know and neither do I. But I do know that you have succeeded admirably in producing a work of painting, of great painting, I mean you have given a vigorous translation into a special language of the truth of lights and shadows and of the reality of objects and creatures.[22]

In 1869 Paul Mantz declared that Manet's works must be accepted independently of their subject. In the same year Ernest Feydeau came out against subject matter and anecdote in painting. The following year Théodore Duret spoke in favour of the artist who, 'having a personal vision of things, succeeds in fixing it on the canvas in an appropriate form which at the same time conveys his personal impression'.[23]

As though in reply to Duret, Claude Monet exhibited at the celebrated Impressionist exhibition of 1874, held in Nadar's studio in the Boulevard des Capucines (an indication, by the way, of the close contacts between photographers and painters), a canvas called *Impression, Rising Sun*. It was in fact on this occasion that a critic coined, mockingly, the term 'Impressionist'. At this exhibition Monet also showed a picture painted from the windows of his friend Nadar's flat, *Le Boulevard des Capucines*. It was obviously inspired by contemporary black-and-white snapshots. His pedestrians are indistinct in the same way as those in Braun's photograph of the Pont des Arts made in 1867.

Monet's passionate interest in the fugitive movement, in what happens in an instant – 'It takes a great effort', he wrote in 1890, 'to succeed in rendering what I am after: instantaneity' – was perhaps awakened by the attempts of photographers to capture movement. But Monet obviously captured movement in colour, the shimmering reflection of lapping water on the white of a boat in motion, the sun trembling on leaves agitated by the wind, reflections of reflections. Monet seems to have followed almost word for word the *Spectator*'s advice of 1842 to artists on how to avoid subservience to photography, 'by imitating the local colour and atmospheric effect' and striving to 'imitate the appearance of movement in figures and foliages, water and cloud'.[24] The earnestness with which Manet and the other Impressionists, as compared with most other painters, tackled problems of colour is to be accounted for, as Charles Chassé puts it in his *Gauguin et son temps*, by their 'wish to steal a march on colour photography, the advent of which had been announced'.[25]

When photography first appeared the enthusiasm was somewhat tempered by its limitation to black and white. People expected to see images recorded in colour as in the *camera obscura*. Indeed Niepce himself was disappointed. From 1850 onwards various more or less successful attempts were made to fix colour, among others by Charles Cros who borrowed one of Manet's paintings for his experiments. Between 1890 and 1900 more methods were devised and considerable progress was made. Finally, in 1907, the brothers Lumière commercialized colour photography.

In 1895 Gauguin said in a Press interview: 'Shall I tell you what will soon be the most faithful work of art? A photograph, when it can render colours, as it will soon be able to. And you would have an intelligent being sweat away for months to achieve the same illusion of reality as an ingenious little machine!'[26]

Monet's concern with problems of light led him to disregard the literary or simply associational side of what he painted. A landscape was for him no more than a succession of colours, relations, values. A woman was a complex of masses from which light was reflected. Monet became a technician of light. For twenty-seven years he painted almost exclusively waterscapes.

Monet's painting is a forerunner of cubism and has had an

influence on non-figurative art. William C. Seitz observes in his *Monet* that the 'fluid structure of the *Cathedrals* looks forward to the flat and pulsating "façades" painted by Braque and Picasso more than fifteen years later'.[27] And Kandinsky, whom many art historians regard as one of the first abstract painters – his earliest non-figurative painting dates apparently from 1910 – recognized Monet's influence on his work:

> Previously [before seeing a Monet haystack at an exhibition in Moscow in 1895] I knew only realistic art ... suddenly, for the first time I saw a *picture*. That it was a haystack the catalogue informed me. I could not recognize it. ... What was revealed to me at that moment was the hitherto unsuspected power of the palette. ... Unconsciously the object was discredited as an indispensable element of the picture.[28]

Cézanne was to say of Monet: 'He is nothing but an eye, but what an eye!'[29] The epigram combines admiration with a grave reproach. Monet used his eye like a photographic lens. And in this sense he had not – and nor had the other Impressionists – detached himself completely from a photographic vision of things. Cézanne, who had originally exhibited with the Impressionists in 1874, finally succeeded, after many years' work, in devising a pictorial technique of space that was fundamentally anti-photographic. He rendered perspective by methods outside the scope of the camera. Thus Cézanne's work is the logical conclusion of the evolution of painting since 1839 and at the same time the point of departure of a large part of modern painting, notably cubism. Cézanne was aware of his position in the history of painting. He wrote: 'I am the primitive of a new art.'

12 □ The artist in the ultimate stage of his evolution

When they had risen above their traditional framework of the Mechanical Arts and become metamorphosed into artists and demi-gods, painters and sculptors discovered that society had not foreseen the emergence of this new type of man. They consequently found themselves living on the fringes of society, and this tended to make them solitary, unstable, eccentric, and subject to fits of depression. They acquired a reputation for being unreliable and unconventional. Some of these traits, which we also find in the artist of our own time, disappeared for nearly two centuries under the influence, in particular, of the Counter-Reformation, which attempted to reintegrate painters and sculptors in society. Romanticism was to see them expelled again, but it also put the finishing touches to the artist's personality by detaching him from everyday reality, making him largely indifferent to the vicissitudes and the sufferings of mankind – the adherents of social art being the exception – and finally by turning him away from reason.

In Chapter 1 we wrote that Proudhon had been one of the very few authors who have dared to denounce the faults of artists. The probable explanation for the caution of other writers is the apparently widespread fear amongst them of the gospel of Beauty in the world. The remarkable thing is that Proudhon's opinions set down in 1863, are still perfectly valid a century later, for the character and the behaviour of artists have not changed a great deal since his day.

They make very large claims to genius and glory. Distinguished, elegant, sensual, greedy, vain, avid for praise and reward, they belong to those who flatter and pay them. They are more often the auxiliaries of corruption that of regeneration. ... In spite of their rich imagination and their ready eloquence, in spite of their colossal vanity, they are unable to answer for themselves or to justify their work. ... The artist lives in isolation, his thoughts are solitary ... he has neither faith nor principles; he is given over to the atheism of his feelings and anarchy of his ideas. He does not know how to make contact with the public. It is a mêlée in which nobody knows himself and everybody pulls his own way. How could they produce works with a popular appeal, they who know nothing about the soul of the people?[1]

Proudhon made no exception for Courbet, whom he judged at his true value: 'He believes himself, like his fellow artists, to be a universal man. This has to be discounted ... he is too often occupied with himself and somewhat ostentatiously vain ... he thinks disjointedly.'[2]

Some years later, in 1886, Zola published his novel, *L'Oeuvre*. He had gradually detached himself from his Impressionist friends whom he had defended so stoutly at the beginning, disappointed, no doubt, by their almost exclusive passion for the technical aspects of painting. Certain traits of the painter Claude Lantier, the hero of the novel, are taken from Manet and Cézanne. Zola describes the inhumanity and the callousness of the artist who devotes his life to the cult of the beautiful. One of the themes he develops is the destruction of woman by art. Many artists' wives, reading Zola's novel, will find in it a reflection of their own lives. In one of the most dramatic scenes the painter succumbs to the aesthetic joy of taking as a model his son who has just died:

The work dried his eyelids, steadied his hand, the cold body of his son was no longer there, there was only a model, a subject the strange nature of which fascinated him. The overdrawn outline of the head, the waxen hue of the flesh, the eyes like openings into the void – all this excited him, warmed him with a kind of flame. He stood back, felt satisfied, smiled vaguely at his work.[3]

The imaginary scene prefigures a real one, that of the death of Claude Monet's wife. Monet picked up his brushes in order to set down a final record of his companion, but the painter soon took over from the husband and he forgot that he had beside him his dead wife to whom he had been devoted. Georges Clemenceau, who was a close friend, relates his confession: 'I caught myself, my eyes fixed on the tragic forehead, trying to work out mechanically the appropriate sequence in the shading off of colour that death had just imposed on the motionless image.'[4]

The theme of *L'Oeuvre* is the life and death by suicide of a painter who suffers from an inability to finish his paintings. Zola's preliminary notes for the novel indicate that Claude Lantier is a neurotic. This clinical observation is of some importance in view of the conclusions Freud was to reach a few decades later. Like Zola he discerned a link between art and neurosis: 'The artist is an introvert on the border of neurosis.'[5] Freud's psychoanalytical theory sheds interesting light on the behaviour of artists. It is applicable especially to late Renaissance and romantic artists – and let us make it clear that for us, modern artists are still romantics. Freud's theory obviously does not apply either to a Giotto or to a Lebrun or to a Chardin. These painters were neither introverts nor neurotics.

What then is the relationship, according to Freud, between neurosis and art? Neurosis and artistic creation are compensatory ways out of psychological distress. The neurotic is an introvert who lives in an imaginary world which he has constructed for himself; it both tortures and delights him but he cannot communicate it to others. The artist is an introvert who wants to 'acquire honour, power, riches, fame and the love of women'.[6] But he belongs to a special category of introverts who avoid neurosis by expressing their fantasies in art. This art appears as a means of communicating aesthetic pleasure to those who suffer feelings of frustration, like the artist himself, but who are not endowed with the 'mysterious power' of art. Art is for the artist a 'way back to reality': he 'wins gratitude and admiration and achieves through his phantasy what at first he attained only in it – honour, power and the love of women'.[7]

But for Freud the artist is not always successful in avoiding neurosis. Like any other man frustrated in real life, he turns away from it and 'transfers all his interest and also his libido to wish-fulfilling phantasies that could lead him to neurosis. Many favourable circumstances are needed if this is not to be the final result of his development. It is well known how often artists suffer from partial inhibitions in their productivity through neurosis.'[8]

Some artists, when afflicted with this 'partial inhibition in their productivity', have recourse to psychoanalysis. In most cases they do not speak about it. They risk the impoverishment or even disappearance of their 'artistic value'. Dr Dracoulidès in his book *Psychanalyse de l'artiste et de son oeuvre,* writes: 'According to Pfister and several other observers the creativeness of an artist who has been psychoanalysed becomes more conscious and more intellectual to the detriment of its artistic values. Sometimes it ceases altogether for, after analysis, real life becomes more satisfying and the life of the imagination contracts.'[9]

In a celebrated line Balzac recognized that a desire satisfied may mean a work not created: 'A woman one sleeps with is a novel one does not write.'[10] There is a parallel between the aesthetic satisfaction procured by artistic creation and the psychological satisfaction procured by the sexual act. 'As soon as sexual desire becomes active,' says Charles Baudoin, 'the aesthetic equilibrium is upset. The sexual instinct excites the imagination in the phase of desire and calms it in the phase of satisfaction.'[11]

Erotic desires that remain unsatisfied gradually induce fear of women and a certain timidity before life. Zola, struck by the importance of frustrated eroticism in Cézanne's life, gave the hero of his novel, Claude Lantier, the same desires and the same fear of love. In his preparatory notes he wrote of Cézanne: 'He was on his guard against women ... he never brought any women to his house and such as he came across he treated as a man who knows nothing about them, concealing pathological shyness under a show of brutality. I don't need women, he used to say, they would disturb me too much.

I simply don't know what they are for, I have always been afraid to try.'[12]

He does not seem to have 'tried' before the age of thirty. To describe an erotic painting by Claude Lantier all Zola had to do was gain stimulus from a canvas that Cézanne had painted in his house in 1867, the *Elopement*. It represents a giant with a bronzed body carrying off a naked woman with long blue-black hair. A whole series of paintings from this period reveal Cézanne's sexual repression. He painted, for instance, a Negro and a white woman both naked lying on a couch and embracing. Another canvas has a naked woman on a sumptuous bed with its curtains drawn back offering her charms to the contemplation of a group of *voyeurs*, among whom can be recognized Cézanne himself.

Cézanne was the typical romantic and bohemian artist who remains shut up in his ivory tower, unstable, irritable, short-tempered, subject to fits of depression and melancholia, solitary, shy but prodigiously proud; he shunned society and all responsibilities; he avoided human contact, even that of his friends; he was hostile to progress and reason, indifferent to the sufferings and the ultimate fate of humanity. For such men art is a refuge, a lifebuoy, a substitute, a compensation.

Cézanne's self-portrait, painted from a photograph, 're-veals', writes John Rewald, in his fascinating book on Cézanne and Zola,

> the painter's state of mind ... he painted himself according to his feelings. By lengthening the chin, giving more relief to the cheeks, accentuating the eyebrows and changing completely the expression of the eyes, Cézanne transformed the gentle and quiet youth of the photograph into a fierce man whose ... piercing look had something menacing about it. This document bears witness to the painter's uneasy spirit, tormented by doubts.[13]

'Those who saw him at the time,' says Joachim Gasquet, 'have described him to me as terrible, hallucinated and as though bestial in a kind of toiling divinity.'[14]

He had a compulsive need to shock people with his

language – he swore, and used obscene words – and by his deliberately disordered dress. He did not care for Manet's refined manner. Claude Monet, who thought highly of him, describes how when he appeared at the Café Guerbois, one of the regular resorts of the Impressionists, he would enter and scrutinize the assembly with a suspicious eye. Then, 'pushing back his jacket with a raffish movement of the hips, he would pull up his trousers and adjust his red belt in the sight of all. After which he shook everybody by the hand. But in front of Manet he would take off his hat and snuffle with his smile: "I'll not shake your hand, Monsieur Manet. I haven't washed for a week."'[15] He would then go and sit in a corner. But if he heard someone 'expressing an opinion too unlike his own, he would get up suddenly and, instead of replying, would leave without saying goodbye to anybody'.[16]

Even more than Cézanne, Gauguin is the prototype of the artist that we know and have to endure today. In him the evolution of the artist reached its ultimate stage. In Gauguin's behaviour – as in that of most modern artists – there was a mixture of spontaneity and calculation. In the hierarchy of the religion of Art he wanted to be at the summit, to function as its high priest and prophet. He could even quite consciously contemplate martyrdom; his wife reproached him with this. He admired Mallarmé, the famous symbolist poet who often helped him and 'died a martyr to art'.[17] When some of his friends advised him to leave Tahiti and go back to France, where it would be easier to treat his numerous ailments, he replied fervently that he would stay in the Islands because 'any revolution generally needs martyrs'[18] (in this case he meant a revolution in painting). He was so engrossed with his religious role that in at least two of his paintings he identified himself with Christ. In the *Christ in Gethsemane*, in which he sought to represent the 'crushing of an ideal, a suffering as much divine as human', he lent his own features to the Man of Sorrows. In another painting of Christ on Golgotha he represented himself as a convict in a white shirt wide-open at the neck, between a Tahitian and his wife. And, in case the point of the painting was not clear, he added this caption in the bottom left-hand corner: 'Near Golgotha'.

His sense of vocation naturally led him to keep his own feelings in check. When he heard of his daughter's death he wrote that this piece of news did not move him in the least, 'inured as I have long since become to suffering'.[19] His wretched family was a burden to him, an obstacle in the accomplishment of his mission. 'My family will have to get by without me.'[20] 'Your wife is dying, that reminds me of mine who is not.'[21] Nowadays when artists want to abandon their wives and families, they invoke the name of Gauguin.

In point of fact, Gauguin's sufferings were not nearly as great as he made out in his letters, for he exaggerated his sufferings in order to win the sympathy of his correspondents so that he could ask them to have money sent to him. The misery he described was part of a legend he was carefully building up with the help of friends. One of the most faithful of these, the symbolist poet Charles Morice, who orchestrated the propaganda in Paris on behalf of Gauguin, admitted quite openly that the painter 'had been at pains to create his own legend, to withdraw from his contemporaries into the distance of the immemorial'. Morice added: 'His purpose was served by a set of circumstances that may indeed have suggested it to him.'[22]

When, in a moment of weakness, Gauguin thought of returning to France, the painter Daniel de Monfreid advised him strongly against it:

It is to be feared that your arrival would disturb a process, an incubation that is taking place in public opinion with regard to yourself. At the moment you are the legendary, unique artist sending from the heart of Oceania his disconcerting and inimitable works, the definitive works of a great man who has disappeared, as it were, from the world ... you enjoy the immunity of the great ones after death ... you have passed into the history of art.[23]

Not unlike the hagiographers of the high Middle Ages, who stylized their lives of saints into uncritical panegyrics, the art historians have told and sung the life of Gauguin as that of a genius of art. ... They have made people believe that he followed a predestined course and chose to abandon the security of a bourgeois job – he was employed by an exchange agent in Paris – in order to devote himself body and soul to the vocation of artist. Such is the legend. The truth is more prosaic. Gauguin, together with many others, found himself out of a job after the crash of the Union Générale in 1882.

Gauguin is also credited with being the sympathetic and magnanimous artist who vigorously championed the cause of the Tahitian natives against an oppressive colonial administration. Also part of the legend. In point of fact, Gauguin defended with zeal the interests of certain colonialists against others who were actually doing what they could to improve the lot of the native population. Again, it is maintained that during his stay in the Pacific islands Gauguin lived in destitution, the victim of shameless exploitation by dealers like Ambroise Vollard. Legend, yet again. Gauguin often had considerable sums at his disposal. It is known that in 1902 he cashed 6,100 gold francs (roughly 15,000 NF) and at the end of his life Vollard was paying him a monthly allowance of 350 francs (roughly 900 NF).

The word 'useful' occurs frequently in Gauguin's letters. He judged others primarily in terms of the benefits he could derive from their activities in his favour. He thought nothing of abandoning a devoted friend who suffered the misfortune of being no longer able to serve his purposes. He was constantly on the lookout for schemes to 'promote' his painting and to put up the prices of his pictures. In March 1895 he wrote from Paris: 'I was fighting a battle to get high quotations for my canvasses and I was spreading rumours of departure to give my pictures rarity value.'[24]

He took every advantage of the climate of speculation prevailing amongst purchasers of modern paintings at the time. He was himself an inveterate speculator. In one year he is said to have made 40,000 gold francs (100,000 NF) on the Stock Exchange, by contemporary standards a fabulous sum. A worker's wage at the time was 25 centimes an hour.

One of the schemes he devised in order to promote his paintings and guarantee a substantial income for himself was to bring together fifteen people who understand my painting or want to make money; make them the following proposal: every year I will send (and in advance) fifteen good canvasses ... like my previous ones ... several drawings at my discretion. For these the fifteen participants will let me have 2,400 francs per annum which makes 160 per person. The pictures will be distributed by drawing lots to determine who should have the first, second etc., choice. It is certain that at this price my canvasses will not be expensive and that within a fairly short time the buyers will not lose.[25]

This particular project was not carried out, but others were and very successfully; for instance, the public auction of Gauguin's works in 1891. To cover the expenses of a trip to Tahiti and a stay on this distant island, Gauguin had the idea of organizing a large sale at the Hôtel Drouot. It was carefully prepared by a Press campaign for which he enlisted the aid of his symbolist friends. Thanks to the personal intervention of Mallarmé, Octave Mirbeau arranged for a 'resounding article' to appear in *L'Echo de Paris*. The piece was reproduced in the sale catalogue and attracted crowds to the Hôtel Drouot. Success was thus ensured and the sale made nearly 10,000 gold francs.

Gauguin's decision to go to the South Seas was partly the outcome of a romantic desire to find an idyllic primitive world far removed from, and uncontaminated by, the materialistic civilization of Europe; but there was also an element of calculating self-interest in it. 'I am rather of Vincent [Van Gogh]'s opinion: the future belongs to painters of the tropics which have not so far been painted. The stupid buying public needs something new by way of subject matter.'[26]

And it is this duality – in which idealism and calculation constantly rub shoulders – that we encounter repeatedly in the majority of modern artists.

13 □ Modern art: an expression of Western decadence

In Chapter 11 we saw how Niepce's discovery provoked in painting a tendency towards non-photographic reality. A parallel influence was that of symbolism. The two together brought about, towards 1886, the birth of modern painting properly so called.

The year 1886 in a sense marks the end of Impressionism. It saw the last exhibition of the Impressionists as a group, the publication by Jean Moréas of his *Symbolist Manifesto* and the launching, by Moréas and others, of the review *Le Décadent*. To contemporaries the two terms were more or less synonymous. Gustave Kahn wrote: 'Although all labels are beside the point, we should nevertheless, for the sake of accuracy, remind all interested parties that decadent is pronounced symbolist.'[1] In fact symbolism is a phase, an important turning point, in the decadence of Western Europe and of France in particular. It is obvious, therefore, that the art that derived from symbolism cannot but be decadent.

The problem of decadence began to attract the interest of literary circles in France towards the middle of the nineteenth century. From then onwards the word recurs more and more frequently. Some writers thought they could discern literary parallels between Roman society of the Late Empire and their own, and this pleased them. Théophile Gautier in his introduction of 1868 to *Les Fleurs du Mal*, written after Baudelaire's death, presents the poet as one of decadence: 'These far from primitive tastes explain themselves and should not be difficult to understand in a decadent poet, author of *Les Fleurs du Mal*.'[2]

This decadent style is the final expression of the word, in

which it is called upon to express everything and taken to the limit of excess. One could recall in this connection the language of the Late Roman Empire marbled already with the green streaks of decay, and the complicated refinements of the Byzantine school, the ultimate form of Greek art fallen into deliquescence.[3]

Théophile Gautier is right: Baudelaire was a decadent poet. Baudelaire could have said the same of Gautier, to whom, in fact, he dedicated Les Fleurs du Mal: 'To the impeccable poet, the perfect magician of French letters'.

In the years after 1830, while some of the leading romantics were abandoning Romanticism for social art, Théophile Gautier for his part was developing the ideas of Romanticism so as to fashion his own theories of art for art's sake. By so doing he watered the seeds of decadence which were already in gestation in Romanticism. Baudelaire was to be the first flower of this efflorescence. 'We are living,' wrote Baudelaire in 1855, 'in a proud age that believes itself to be above the misadventures of Greece and Rome.'[4] What he certainly did not realize was that he was himself going to contribute to the misadventures of our society and to its intellectual decline.

Baudelaire widened the gulf between art on the one hand, and morals and science on the other. 'Poetry,' he wrote, 'cannot on pain of death and downfall be assimilated to science or to morals.'[5] He refused to call George Sand an artist, on the ground that she moralized: 'She has always been a moralist ... she has therefore never been an artist. ... The fact that several men managed to become enamoured of this latrine only shows how low men of this age have sunk.'[6] No cause must be defended, no doctrine upheld except, of course, that of independent art. Baudelaire became very angry with a certain Wiertz, a painter who presumed to have ideas, 'unspeakable puffer, charlatan, idiot, thief! He believes he has a destiny to accomplish.' Indignant and aghast, Baudelaire compared him to Victor Hugo, that other humanitarian: 'Wiertz and Hugo want to save mankind!'[7] Baudelaire's own shocking attitude made him a passive and indifferent spectator of the exploitation of man by man.

This contempt for humanity naturally went hand in hand with a profound contempt for democracy and a marked preference for what is known as 'strong' government, a sentiment shared by the majority of the supporters of art for art's sake, and subsequently by the symbolists. 'What a ruthless dictatorship is that of opinion in democratic societies.'[8] 'Aristocratic government is the only reasonable and stable one. Monarchy or republic, based on democracy, are equally absurd.'[9]

Baudelaire had little use for the masses. In *Mon coeur mis à nu* he wrote: 'Among men only the poet, the priest and the soldier are great. The man who sings, the man who sacrifices and the man who sacrifices himself. The rest are good for the whip. Let us beware of the people, of common sense, of the heart, of inspiration and of the obvious.'[10] Baudelaire's hostility towards democracy and the masses went with a violent hostility towards science and progress: 'What could be more absurd than progress ... the belief in progress is a doctrine for the lazy.'[11]

He wanted art to be independent not only of science and morals but also of nature. This aspect of his doctrine must be emphasized because one of the characteristics of modern art is precisely its independence with regard to nature. The principal consequence of this doctrine was to pave the way for all modern art's deformations of reality – from Gauguin to Pop Art, by way of Picasso.

The poet of *Les Fleurs du Mal* denounced the romantic cult of nature professed by Jean-Jacques Rousseau, who made the contrast in his writings between depraved man and the virtuous man of primitive societies. In the fight against this love of nature Baudelaire was preceded by the Marquis de Sade, of whom he wrote with respect: 'One must always go back to de Sade – that is to say to natural man – in order to explain evil.' For Baudelaire, nature is perverse and ugly: it drives us to kill our fellow creatures. What is natural lacks both beauty and morality. Thus 'trade is natural, therefore it is vile. ... Woman is natural, therefore abominable.'[12] Art must be as remote as possible from nature. Nature is monotonous and banal. 'I should like meadows to be tinted red, rivers golden yellow and trees painted blue. Nature has no imagination.'[13] The poet's vision was to be realized by Gauguin.

Baudelaire thus came to proclaim that the artificial was superior to the natural – the musical box to the nightingale, the woman who wore make-up to a country madonna. 'For me a woman is beautiful only if she has kohl eye-shadow, make-up on her face and lipstick on her lips.'[14] On one occasion he dyed his own hair green. He was attracted by what was against nature and attached value to depravity – defined by Gautier as 'divergence from the normal type, something that animals led necessarily by immutable instinct are incapable of'.[15] In this he makes common ground with de Sade.

Seventeen years after Baudelaire's death, in 1884, J. K. Huysmans published his novel, *A rebours*. It had a considerable impact and its hero, Des Esseintes, came to be regarded in literary circles as the archetypal decadent. He devotes his life to a struggle by any means he can imagine against nature. The work is a sustained denunciation of nature and a hymn to the glory of artificiality. Des Esseintes sleeps in the daytime and lives at night, prefers artificial light to that of the sun, artificial flowers to real ones, mechanical fish to goldfish. He matches the colour of his socks with that of his feelings and discerns correspondences between curaçao and the clarinet, kümmel and the oboe. He reaches the stage of feeding himself by enema, 'an insult thrown in the face of old nature'.[16] Some of the themes of *A rebours* derive from Baudelaire, such as the correspondence between colours and states of mind, and between colours, sounds and smells.

The years which followed the appearance of *A rebours* were to witness a veritable onslaught on naturalism by a whole army of novelists and poets: J. K. Huysmans himself, Paul Verlaine, Jean Moréas, Gustave Kahn, Stéphane Mallarmé, Charles Morice, Octave Mirbeau and Albert Aurier. Charles Baudelaire – along with Arthur Rimbaud – was recognized by common consent as one of the most influential pioneers of the decadent movement which, as we have seen, took the name of 'Symbolism'.

There were other influences – Schopenhauer and Hegel. The French translation of Hegel's *Vorlesungen über die Asthetik* appeared in a second edition in 1875. For Hegel too the object of art is not to imitate nature: 'what is the good of reproducing what nature already offers to our gaze? This puerile task, unworthy of the mind that addresses itself to it, unworthy of the man who undertakes it, can only end by revealing to him his own impotence and the vanity of his efforts. For the copy will always remain inferior to the original.'[17] This doctrine amounts to a condemnation not only of the traditional art of animal, landscape and history painters but also social art, and Impressionism, which in certain of its aspects did not abandon the imitation of nature.

Hegel goes on to develop at length his own theory of what constitutes a true work of art. We cannot enter into this here and will confine ourselves to mentioning a few elements that became the common property of art criticism and, in particular, were taken up by the symbolists: the role of the Spirit in art; the importance of the Idea in relation to form; form as the symbolic expression of the Idea; the notion that reality is a manifestation of the spiritual.

In his manifesto of 1886 Jean Moréas defined the aims and the methods of Symbolism as follows:

Symbolic poetry tries to clothe the idea in a sensuous form which, however, is not to be thought of as an end in itself; serving to express the Idea the form should remain subordinate to it. The Idea in its turn must not allow itself to be deprived of the sumptuous simars of external analogies; for the essential character of symbolic art consists in never going as far as the conception of the Idea in itself.[18]

The notion common to all symbolist intellectuals of the period was that of expressing not an image of the external world but the self of the writer or the artist. What counted was not the objects that surround us but the way they are interpreted by individual minds and sensibilities. In relation to the thinking man, everything external to the self only existed according to his own conception of it.

For artists and men of letters, the universe was henceforth simply a projection outside itself of the human psyche in so far as it participates in being. Poetry, far from presenting psychological truth must present psychic truth, for it was nothing other than the 'materialization of a quasi-mystical experience, the expression of an ineffable message'. As for art, its task was to discover the hidden meaning of objects which were for the artist symbols of an existence at a deeper level, and to trace correspondences between the visible and the invisible. It was envisaged as a system of transpositions in which forms and colours were used to suggest thoughts and feelings. Music was recognized as one of the supreme means of suggestion. Poets sought in it a stimulus to creative reverie and attended to sound and rhythm as a source of images. Verlaine demanded 'music before all else'[19] and Mallarmé defined symbolist poetry as follows: 'The expression through human language brought back to its essential rhythm of the mysterious sense of aspects of existence.'[20]

Mallarmé, the unchallenged master of Symbolism, is the poet in the ultimate stage of his evolution. He is the decadent writer *par excellence*. Des Esseintes considers the poet with 'Byzantine refinements', as he calls Mallarmé, to be the most decadent of them all, more so than Baudelaire, Barbey d'Aurévilly, Verlaine or Edmond de Goncourt. Like Des Esseintes, Mallarmé had a special taste for the late Latin poets. 'The literature from which my mind will expect delight is the expiring poetry of the last moments of Rome.'[21] In his book *La France Byzantine*, Julien Benda denounced the irrationality of Mallarmé, a poet with a passion for the hermetic and the esoteric, who is said to have envisaged founding a secret society of poets. Mallarmé's passion for language recalls that of the Alexandrian poets. Benda also castigated the irrationality and the decadence – though the word 'decadent' itself practically disappeared from the literary vocabulary after 1890 – of writers who were steeped in Mallarmé and symbolism: Valéry, Claudel, Gide, Proust, Giraudoux, and Eluard.

Shut up in an ivory tower more remote from the world than

that of the romantics, Mallarmé attempted to write poetry so obscure that it could only be understood by a few initiates. He was often afraid of making himself too clear. Art was intended for an élite who must devote their lives to it entirely. Life must be sacrificed to art. This religion of Art, of the Beautiful – or of aesthetics – was to be one for a small number of the elect. Thus the divorce between art and the public became complete.

In 1891 a literary critic, Jules Huret, made a survey of the literary situation. Mallarmé, a contributor, declared:

To name an object is to do away with three-quarters of the enjoyment of a poem which consists in the pleasure of guessing little by little; the great thing is to suggest the object. ... If a person of middling intelligence and insufficient literary preparation chances to open a book written in this way and claims to enjoy it, something has gone wrong, things must be put back where they belong. There should always be an enigma in poetry; the purpose of literature and it is the only one – is to evoke objects.[22]

The main purpose of Huret's survey was to seek the opinion of the best known writers – sixty-four were questioned on the current position of naturalism, of which Zola was the chief luminary. The replies showed that the majority of the writers, even some of Zola's disciples, considered naturalism to be a dead letter. The condemnation of naturalism carried with it the condemnation, in varying degrees, of realism, reason, progress, science and democracy. Symbolism was acclaimed as the movement of the day.

In painting, a somewhat analogous movement was developing with artists like Puvis de Chavannes, Odilon Redon and Gustave Moreau in opposition to such naturalism and realism as still survived in the painting of the Impressionists. The symbolists were looking for a standard-bearer in the realm of the plastic arts, and their choice fell upon Gauguin. Gauguin accepted the role: there were, in fact, numerous points of contact between him and the symbolists. But he remained independent and did not adopt all the theories of the symbolists systematically; indeed there were some which he did not understand very well. In accepting, he also reckoned with the possibility of receiving financial aid from these writers and here he was not disappointed.

Also in 1891, in connection with the sale organized in aid of Gauguin and morally sponsored by Mallarmé, a young critic, Albert Aurier, published what amounted to a manifesto of pictorial symbolism, in which he proclaimed Gauguin the leader of symbolic art. A year earlier Aurier had written an enthusiastic article on Van Gogh celebrating him as a symbolist. Aurier saw Symbolism in opposition to Impressionism which he considered to be nothing but a 'variation on realism'.[23] The mystical tone of the 'manifesto' – 'mysticism alone can save our society from the crassness of sensualism and utilitarianism' – angered the Impressionists, particularly Camille Pissarro who was under no illusions about the anti-democratic and anti-populist mystical attitude of the symbolists. 'They must be fought like the plague,' he wrote to his son.[24]

The symbolists were mystics who accorded primacy to dreams, to the subconscious, to the imagination and intuition. They were hostile to clarity, logic and positivism. Many of them became interested in other doctrines, each more mystical than the last, which appeared, or reappeared at the time, and some of which are still with us today: obscurantist and pseudo-scientific pursuits like astrology, alchemy, occultism, and spiritualism. The magazine Le Décadent stated in 1886 that 'neurosis, hysteria, charlatanism in science and extremist Schopenhauerism are the premonitory symptoms of social evolution'.[25]

According to Aurier the artist must disengage himself from objects and express ideas: 'Objects that is to say, in abstract terms, the various combinations of lines, planes, shadows and colours constitute the vocabulary of a mysterious but miraculously expressive language which one must know in order to be an artist.'[26] 'The artist is entitled to exaggerate, to attenuate, to deform shapes, lines and colours not only according to his personal vision, according to the moulds of his personal subjectivity, as happens sometimes even in realist art, but

more than this to exaggerate, attentuate and deform them as
the Idea to be expressed requires.'[27] For Aurier there was also
another, less 'philosophical' reason why artists should treat
shapes, lines and colours in this way, and that was the menac-
ing presence of the camera. It was his wish and his hope that
painters would avoid anything remotely suggestive of photography. He reached this position probably as a result of his
conversation with Gauguin who, as we have seen, was very
much aware of the competition offered by the camera.
Gauguin's merit and achievement in this domain, as he himself realized, was to anticipate certain improvements of the
photographic plate, particularly in relation to colour.

The ideas of Aurier and the symbolists were taken up and
disseminated by Maurice Denis, a painter and theoretician of
art, and one of the founders of the Nabi movement, in a series
of articles he wrote in 1890 and the following years which
were much read and studied in the world of avant-garde
painting in France and elsewhere. He proclaimed that: 'The
painter's subject is in himself. ... All spectacles, all emotions,
all dreams resolve themselves for him into combinations of
patches; into relationships of tones and tints; into lines.'[28]

It may be noted here that Delacroix had had a remarkable
presentiment of the future when he apostrophized the young
painter in search of a subject: 'The subject is in yourself, your
impressions in front of nature.'[29]

Maurice Denis also wrote: 'All art consists in representing
ourselves, in evoking states of mind, I believe, in symbolism,
in the theory that asserts the possibility of expressing human
emotions and thoughts through aesthetic correspondences
and equivalences in beauty.'[30] Denis too was emphatic in his
advice to painters to keep away from photography. This
theme, as with Aurier, recurs many times in his writings.

The symbolists and Gauguin shared a feeling of hostility
and scorn for the materialistic civilization of the West. The
former chose to withdraw into hermetism and artificiality, the
latter into exile and primitivism. Artificiality is primitivism in
reverse. This primitivism was preparing the ground for
Douanier Rousseau and the appreciation of negro sculpture.

Gauguin wanted his painting to stimulate the imagination like music; to be suggestive and dream-evoking. He cared little about imitating the tones of nature. He wanted colours to express his feelings and sensations. He made Baudelaire's dream come true by painting red fields, yellow trees and pink-grey dogs. He established correspondence between his thoughts and his paintings.

In 1888 and 1905 two new movements appeared in painting: the Nabis (Denis, Sérusier, Bonnard, Vuillard) and the Fauves (Matisse, Marquet, Vlaminck, Derain). Both explored further the deformation of nature. But it is above all with Picasso and his painting *Les Demoiselles d'Avignon* (1907) that the deformation of reality entered a new stage of development.

The symbolism and decadence of the intellectual circles of Barcelona and Paris at the turn of the century were among the formative factors of Picasso's early years – perhaps the decisive ones for the subsequent development of his painting. They have been convincingly identified by Phoebe Pool and Anthony Blunt in their book *Picasso: the Formative Years*. When Picasso reached Barcelona in 1895 the 'modernist' intellectuals with whom he was going to associate were passionately opposed to realism and considered naturalism obsolete. They shared the predilection of the French decadents for the abnormal, the sickly, the erotic, the unbalanced, the macabre and the pathological. Primitivism was the order of the day. Verlaine and Mallarmé were looked up to in this milieu. Schopenhauer and Hegel were read; so was Nietzsche. The young painters preferred Moreau, Carrière and Puvis de Chavannes to the Impressionists. They were familiar with the theories of Maurice Denis. A drawing of 1899 by Picasso documents this *fin de siècle* climate in Barcelona. It is a portrait of his friend, Jaime Sabarthès, and in the top right-hand corner are the words '*Poeta decadente*'. In Paris, which he visited frequently from 1900 onwards and where he finally settled in 1904, Picasso attracted the notice of Jean Moréas and was soon adopted by a group of decadent young writers and art critics – we use the term 'decadent' to define them, though they did not accept the label themselves – Max Jacob, Maurice Raynal, André Salmon, and Guillaume Apollinaire. He also met Alfred Jarry.

The anti-naturalist atmosphere in which Picasso had lived since his adolescence prepared him for the decisive step in the decomposition of forms. The ever present menace of the camera also helped to prepare the ground for this pictorial revolution. Picasso later recognized it: 'Why should the artist insist on rendering what can be fixed so well with the aid of the camera. It would be folly, would it not? Photography came at just the right moment to free the painter from litera- ture, from anecdote, even from subject matter itself. Should not painters take advantage of the freedom they have re- covered to do something else?'[31] But in fact it was seeing the forms of primitive sculpture, Iberian and Negro, that decided Picasso on the step that led to complete deformation. The result, as is well-known, was *Les Demoiselles d'Avignon*; and consequent on it, the cubism of Braque and later of Léger, Gris, Picabia and Delaunay.

The idea of astonishing the public was probably not absent from Picasso's mind when he painted *Les Demoiselles d'Avignon*. And the desire to surprise is a factor not to be underestimated by anyone who wishes to understand the evolution of modern painting in the twentieth century, with its ever more rapid succession of 'isms': cubism, orphism, simultaneism, purism, musicalism, futurism, rayonism, suprematism, magic realism, verism, dadaism, surrealism, non-figurative symbolism, neoplasticism, brutalism, tachism, synthetism, abstract expressionism, and so forth – not to mention the swarm of movements with no 'ism' to their names: naive art, primitive art, non-figurative art, concrete art, *art brut*, action painting, *art informel*, hard edge, kinetic art, pop art, op art, self-destructive art. The list is far from complete and it can only become less so.

The modern artist's need to astonish the public has its origins in the romantic desire to shock, to *épater le bourgeois*. Baudelaire admired in dandyism the 'last fling of heroism in periods of decadence ... the pleasure of astonishing others and the proud satisfaction of never being astonished oneself'.[32] He will even go further and add that 'a little charlatanism is always permitted to genius – it is like make-up on the cheeks of a naturally beautiful woman'.[33] From charlatanism it is but a step to mystification. The symbolists became mystics. As Charles Chassé puts it in his *Les Clefs de Mallarmé* (in which he supplies the key to Mallarmé's pornographic poems – Littré's dictionary), 'in the symbolist period there was a need not only to mystify others but also to be mystified oneself'.[34] Jarry is a classic example. He was to admit one day that 'his' *Ubu-Roi* was no more than a schoolboy's hoax of which he does not seem even to have been the author. It is known that he made a profound impression on Picasso. Apollinaire in his turn, succeeded Jarry as master mystifier. 'Nobody,' writes Thibaudet, 'had greater imaginative resources in mystification than Guillaume Apollinaire.'[35]

These born mystifiers are sometimes beaten at their own game. The success of some of the names they launch surprise them. An example of this is Douanier Rousseau, whose paintings reveal the mental age of a child. The figures and objects in his paintings are all deformed. He respects neither anatomy nor perspective. But the way for his success had been prepared by the fact that, ever since Gauguin, painters, in their hatred of logic and science, had been trying to return to the first lispings of children and primitive peoples. In Douanier Rousseau they were interested to discover an adult European who painted like a child and a primitive. Gauguin was also a mystifier. He managed apparently to convince Rousseau that the latter had been decorated by the President of the Republic and that, therefore, an expression of thanks was due. On one occasion he said to Sérusier: 'I know two things which can never be ridiculous: a child and a savage.'[36] And Van Gogh reported: 'Gauguin and Bernard talk now of doing child painting.'[37] Picasso who also mystified Rousseau at a celebrated banquet, but bought one of his pictures, confessed to Herbert Read at an exhibition of children's drawing: 'When I was their age I could draw like Raphael but it took me a lifetime to learn to draw like them.'[38]

The deliberate attempt by modern artists to recapture the inarticulateness of children, to give primacy to the subconscious and to reject the despised inheritance of Western civilization has resulted during the past half-century in the 'creation' throughout the world of thousands of paintings and other artefacts each more incongruous than the last. The acceptance they have won offers incontrovertible proof that the critical spirit of the West is in retreat.

In 1912 Picasso stuck old newspaper cuttings on a canvas; Braque, in the same year, strips of tapestry simulating wood; and Juan Gris, a fragment of a looking-glass. In Russia Tatlin attached a tin box among various pieces of wood and broken glass to a badly squared plank (1914). In Berlin Schwitters composed his masterpieces with refuse retrieved from rubbish bins – old shoe soles, bits of shoe lace, iron wires, rags, feathers, pens, cheese paper, used tramcar tickets (1919). Duchamp set a bicycle wheel with the fork downwards on a kitchen stool (1913), inscribed a comb with these meaningless words: 'Three or four drops of height have nothing to do with savagery' (1916) and sent a urinal to the Salon des Indépendants in New York (1917).

After this catalogue of bizarre objects, sacred relics of the religion of aesthetics, one hardly dares mention that between 1910 and 1914 four easel painters, four high priests of the religion of Art, succeeded not simply in deforming nature but in doing away with it altogether by the invention of non-figurative painting: Kandinsky in Germany, Delaunay in France, Mondrian in Holland and Malevich in Russia. The last-named painted in 1913 a black square on a white background.

Since this heroic age artists have had to show a great deal of imaginative resource – Baudelaire would have admired them for that – to outdo these pioneering feats, to regress further along the road away from civilization towards childhood and primitivism. Their achievement should not go unrecognized. They have succeeded so well that it is often difficult to tell their work from that of children and primitives, sometimes even from that of the mentally ill. Stranger still, some modern painters have adopted a style similar to that of the celebrated anthropoid artists like Sophie, the gorilla of Rotterdam, or Congo the chimpanzee of London. Coherent thought having been banished from artistic creation, it has often become impossible to distinguish between sculptures and objects picked up at random. (In 1960 a painting machine was devised which 'imagined' paintings similar to those of contemporary artists.)

Not content with deforming their works, artists have even set about destroying them – as a means of creation – with knives (Fontana), rifles (Niki de Saint-Phalle), flame-throwers (Yves Klein); they have had car bodies crushed in industrial presses (César), thrown violins from the sixth floor on to the courtyard pavement (Arman), or simply jumped with both feet on old objects made of worm-eaten wood (Ralph Ortiz). These holy men of art have found in London, the city which has inherited from Paris the sceptre of art and of decadence, an evangelizing theorist of destruction, Gustave Metzger. With barbarous refinement Metzger launched in 1959 a manifesto of self-destruction in which he proclaimed the absolute necessity for artists to imagine works capable of destroying themselves within a lapse of time varying from a few instants to a few years, twenty at the most.

Gustave Metzger had the idea of destroying a nylon canvas with hydrochloric acid, John Latham of burning carefully selected books stacked up in the form of a tower. But it is Tinguély – who set up auto-destructive machines in the garden of the Museum of Modern Art in New York – who has gone furthest: by dynamiting a work of art, made with patience and love, up in the Nevada desert.

Yoko Ono has proposed the self-destruction of artists:

> Use your blood to paint.
> Keep painting until you faint.
> Keep painting until you die.[39]

No artist has so far accomplished his own self-destruction.

14 □ The religion of Art in the capitalist economy

As we approach the year 2000, the religion of Art has become the most dynamic one in the West, especially in the United States. Millions of men and women across the Atlantic have been converted to it in recent years. A minority cult so far, it is in the process of becoming a majority one. This extraordinary vitality cannot be understood without reference to the close links that have developed between art and capitalism.

In Chapter 7 we tried to show how pictures had become an excellent investment, with the security of gold itself, and how financial crises caused fluctuations on the art market. In this chapter we shall indicate how works of art have been turned into stocks and shares and how the American tax laws have contributed to the integration of the religion of Art into the capitalist economy.

Zola's *L'Oeuvre* offers a glimpse of the changes that were taking place in the contemporary art market, particularly in relation to the Impressionists – pictures beginning to be looked upon in stock-exchange terms, bankers intervening at critical moments, the mechanism for 'launching' painters and, a fact worthy of especial notice, the preponderant role of the well-known Impressionist dealer, Paul Durand-Ruel (in Zola's novel he is called Naudet), in the evolution of the market. These facts, particularly the interventions of bankers in the financing of Durand-Ruel, are confirmed by Lionello Venturi in *Les Archives de l'Impressionisme*. We read in *L'Oeuvre*:

> Naudet ... was a dealer who for some years had been revolutionizing the picture trade. ... He was changing the market completely by forcing out of it the collector of

taste and dealing only with moneyed clients who knew nothing about art and bought pictures as shares of stock either out of vanity or in the hope that they would appreciate.[1]

There was talk of a syndicate, of an understanding with bankers to keep up the high prices 'and bankruptcy seemed to be the inevitable end of these stock-exchange operations, a leap into the excess and the lies of speculation'.[2]

The state of affairs reflected in Zola's novel worried artists. It reminded Van Gogh of the wild speculation in tulip bulbs in Holland in the seventeenth century. In 1885 he wrote to his brother: 'It is no use trying to get me out of my pessimism about the picture trade ... I see this peculiar interference with prices in painting more and more as a sort of traffic rather like the one in tulips.'[3]

Pissarro in a letter of 10 July 1887 expressed gloom: 'The collector today regards a painting only as a share of stock, it is disgusting to be part of such a degenerate business.'[4] And in another one, of 13 April 1891, he thought Durand-Ruel was acting like a speculator: 'The lower the prices the better for him – he can leave our canvasses to his children. He behaves like a modern speculator for all his angelic sweetness.'[5]

In fact it was not the passion for speculating that made Durand-Ruel into so revolutionary a force in the picture market but what Venturi called his 'excessive craving for power'. To satisfy his ambition he transformed the relationship between the artist, the Salon and the collector. His practice of setting up a trust with a painter's pictures condemned the Salon to eventual disappearance and gave the acquisition of pictures the character of a stock investment irrespective of the individual buyer's intentions. By monopolizing the production of a living painter – buying up his old works and pre-empting his future ones against the guarantee of a monthly allowance, Durand-Ruel hoped to be able to control prices. Like any monopolist he hoped to force them up and protect them from the fluctuations of supply and demand by limiting the number of canvasses on the market and promoting them by skilful propaganda.

To control the output of several painters in this way required financial resources far beyond anything a contemporary dealer, however wealthy, could muster. Not only was it necessary to buy up all the paintings of each of the artists concerned but sometimes to buy a number of them at an inflated price in order to maintain the artist's market value in case other works of his came up for sale from collections, for family or other reasons.

Thus, shortly before the war of 1870, Durand-Ruel was looking for financial support. He wrote about this to one of his friends: 'to find a capitalist prepared to help me ... so that I could keep the superb works in my possession and not be pressed to sell them (which is always bad and prevents prices being kept up). He spoke to me about Edwards, a Levantine baker who has been living in Paris for some years and who made a large fortune in Constantinople.'[6] Edwards agreed to advance capital to Durand-Ruel; we do not know at what rate of interest (Durand-Ruel subsequently called it 'usurious') against a number of pictures as surety. Durand-Ruel could now launch his project of a painter's trust. He financed a review to publicize the value of his stock. But neither the money nor the propaganda proved enough. Prices rose too slowly to cover the interest on the loan and the pictures deposited with Edwards could not be retrieved.

Convinced that his project was basically sound, Durand-Ruel began to look for another capitalist to finance him. It took him several years to discover one. Finally, in 1880 Feder, a banker who collected pictures and was a director of the powerful Société de l'Union Générale, placed at his disposal sufficient funds to allow him to redeem the pictures left in bond with Edwards and 'go back into business in a fruitful manner'. But luck was not on his side. On 2 February 1882 the Union Générale collapsed in ruins causing a veritable cataclysm in the world of finance and the stock exchange. Durand-Ruel, obliged to refund the bank, found himself in great financial straits – in 1884 he was over 1 million gold francs (3,000,000 NF) in debt. He was not afloat again until he discovered that the future of the art market lay on the other side of the Atlantic, in the true cradle of capitalism, the United States.

Another well-known victim of the Union Générale crash was Gauguin. As canvasser of an exchange agent, he had become familiar with the milieu from which a large part of Durand-Ruel's clientele was recruited, and had learned to speculate on young painters' works which could be bought at a low price in the expectation that one day they would fetch a high one. Gauguin had been introduced to the stock exchange by Gustave Arosa, a financier and collector who had been buying Pissarros since 1871. For his part Gauguin acquired through the stock exchange paintings by Manet, Pissarro, Degas, Monet, Renoir, Sisley and Cézanne. In 1885 he wrote to Denmark where his wife was looking after his collection to tell her not to start selling too soon or at too low a price: 'I have the pictures in Denmark and the way things are going one day I shall have nothing left. I want to keep my two Cézannes, which are rare of their kind because he only finished a few, and one day will be very valuable. I would rather you sold the Degas drawing but it must be said that he alone is selling a great deal.'[7] In 1888 he was delighted that Monets should be going up: 'It will be one more example of the speculator who compares past prices with present ones. And in this sense it is not exorbitant to ask four hundred francs for a Gauguin if a Monet fetches three thousand.'[8] He took it so much for granted that people collected pictures in order to speculate that he was almost touched when he heard of a painting of his being bought for the love of it: 'Be this as it may I am delighted that Delius now owns it [this picture], as it is not a speculation purchase with a view to reselling but because he likes it.' [9]

It is worth remarking that Gauguin's knowledge of the art market and its connections with the stock exchange made him appreciate the kind of operations Durand-Ruel engaged in: 'And when I was in Paris I sold from two thousand francs down to five hundred at the lowest. No, the truth is that it is the picture-dealer who fixes the prices if he knows how to go about it.'[10] In his last years Gauguin signed an exclusive contract with Vollard who adopted Durand-Ruel's methods of exploiting the market.

In his memoirs, written in old age, Durand-Ruel admitted that a number of his clients speculated. He almost blames them for it but in fact he had encouraged them to do so. Of Larrieu, he says that he had 'always speculated on pictures';[11] of Laurent Richard, that 'like many collectors who are also speculators, he was frightened by the fall in prices about to occur';[12] of Faure, that 'he bought back some superb Corots, taking advantage of lower prices after the death of this great artist', and that he hoped 'to sell easily what he had been able to collect in favourable conditions'.[13] And in another connection: 'The only buyers were always a few rare collectors and a few knowledgeable speculators ready to sell whenever this was profitable.'[14]

Painters learned to live with speculators and financiers and to share their worries about political events – elections, threats of *coups d'état*, war scares – that were likely to affect the Paris Bourse or Wall Street. When the Bourse was shaky, the picture market felt it immediately.

Pissarro's correspondence with his son Lucien shows the importance of national and international crisis in the decisions of collectors to restrain their buying of modern paintings. In February 1887 he writes: 'It is these confounded war rumours that stop everything, collectors dare not buy any more. And yet it is the only investment – since they buy solely for that – that is safe.'[15] And on 15 May of the same year: 'Heymann's collectors lost heavily during the recent crisis, some time will have to elapse before they regain confidence. You must remember that Heymann recruits his collectors from the middle-range capitalists.'[16] Pissarro paid increasing attention to the crisis of American capitalism, the United States having become, thanks to Durand-Ruel, the chief market for Impressionist painting (and for all modern art). On 17 November 1890 he writes: 'The papers here announce a dreadful crash in New York and London.'[17]

On 7 June 1893: 'Joseph [Durand-Ruel's son] has arrived from New York, his reports are very alarming. It seems they expect a real crisis soon as a result of the compromises the Republican Party has made with the big speculators in metals. Although they are not involved in transactions of this kind, the art dealers will be affected by them for some time. Mark my words! It is always the same story: if business slackens we are going to have trouble.'[18]

On 15 July 1894: 'I have such anxieties about the future that I am afraid my paintings will be affected ... in America it is even worse, nothing, nothing! ... Miss Cassatt says it is simply due to the election, and that the situation will be restored when the new team comes in! Which is to say that new pick-pockets will replace the old! ... There is consolation for you!'[19]

Today the fluctuations of the American economy would have given Pissarro less cause for concern, for the government of the United States, having decided that the religion of Art should be protected and encouraged, passed tax laws in its favour, and as a result the market prices of pictures became relatively independent of Wall Street (except, of course, in the event of a major crash like that of 1929).

The purpose of these laws was to attract to museums, the temples of the new religion, its cult objects, works of art. In pursuance of this, 'generous' donors were allowed to claim substantial tax relief. The social consequences of these tax exemptions have been iniquitous: what is in effect a disguised subsidy to the rich who can afford art collections has had to be made up by taxing more heavily those not rich enough to have any, who are thus penalized twice over for not being richer than they are, while they can watch those richer than themselves playing at 'art patrons' with their money.

The fiscal advantages offered were such that – quite apart from the extraordinary privilege of being able to keep the pictures donated in one's house until one dies – large numbers of rich taxpayers who had never taken any notice of modern art except possibly to make fun of it, started to hunt not only for Impressionist and Post-Impressionist paintings but also for works by young artists with promising talents which could still be bought cheap. Some of these new collectors soon discovered that the tax authorities were defenceless and that one could get away with any kind of assessment which allowed fantastic profits. It was only in 1962–3 that the American Treasury put a stop to these frauds, and in 1964 that Congress passed a law obliging donors to part with their donations immediately and not at their death.

Maximum tax relief for donators of works of art is a deduction of 20 per cent from their taxable income, which means that to claim it a picture collector whose annual income is $100,000 has to donate a painting valued at $20,000. He may have bought it for $1,000 or $2,000. The tax collector works on the basis of this valuation and taxes only 80 per cent of his income. Before the Treasury learned to question the valuations of experts, museums often used to have pictures estimated above their market value in order to encourage donations. When a collector is in the category of those paying 90 per cent on their income, it is more in his interest to donate his pictures than to sell them, as there is a 25 per cent tax on capital surplus value.

The system of tax reliefs in the United States has undoubtedly contributed to the rocketing of prices in the modern art market. It is also true that if tomorrow Congress were to abolish them, there would be a world-wide slump in the prices of modern pictures. But even if prices did fall in that way the interest in art in the United States would scarcely be likely to diminish. For as a result of their initiation into the world of artists, critics and museum directors – originally embarked on in a spirit of self-interest – the art collectors have gradually been converted to the religion of Art by the active proselytizing of its apostles. Scales have fallen from their eyes and they have been made to see that a picture is not only a market commodity but also an object of religious devotion. Having thus attained to a new state of grace, these men have learned to commune with the faithful in worshipping at the shrines of this same aesthetic creed.

15 □ Art: an enemy of the people*

Some twenty-five years have elapsed since I wrote *Against Art and Artists* and in that time there has been an increasing conversion of the middle classes to modern art, with the surprising result that the bourgeoisie now happily accepts their children as artists. In fact they are proud of having given birth to inspired individuals.

The development may have been encouraged by the fact that the contemporary artist dresses very much like the rest of the world, and no longer has a particular bohemian lifestyle. The time is past when the artist sought to shock. It was this aggressive attitude on the artists' part that discouraged the nineteenth-century bourgeoisie from making a cult of art. Today, Modern Art has been re-integrated with the art of the Old Masters into one religion, that of Art.

The French bourgeoisie is not the only one to have converted to Art: these days no one at a dinner party dares to say that Picasso or Moore are poking fun at the world. This phenomenon now affects middle-class citizens throughout the Western world. We may well wonder if there is not a correlation betwen the growth of faith in art and the decline in religious observance, political ideology and science. Art is a compensation.

In his book *L'Invention de l'Europe*, Emmanuel Todd gives an account of the 'de-Christiánisation of the years 1730–1800',[1] corresponding to the promotion of taste in the second half of the eighteenth century, evoked in our chapter 'The artist, dealer and critic'. Todd suggests that the final phase of

*The title of this chapter is borrowed from Roger L. Taylor's book *Art, an Enemy of the People* (Brighton, 1978).

de-Christianisation began around 1965. Opinion-polls confirm this trend. 'Generally, attendance at church dropped from 20–25% in the 1960s to 10–15% towards the end of the 1970s.'[2] The figure in the early 1990s is substantially lower than 10%. In France in the age group of 18 to 24 only 2 to 4% go regularly to church. But the decline in traditional religion in Europe was at first succeeded by a rise in ideology. 'Men replaced ... the lost image of the City of God with a new image of an ideal society. ... Social metaphysics replaced religious metaphysics, the visions of an earthly ideal that of the heavenly.'[3] But in their turn, 'between 1965 and 1990, most of the ideological systems of Europe were affected by an inexorable process of decay which destroyed belief, weakened political parties, transformed the nature of political alignments, creating everywhere a sense of emptiness and loss of direction'.[4]

Was it just chance that the ideology of art blossomed during this period of change in people's unconsciousness? It was equally unconsciously that bourgeois society was gradually converted to art.

In the seventeenth century, however, a new mystique had been born: this mystique which expanded in the nineteenth century. It was the origin of those laboratories described by Pasteur as 'The Temples of the Future and of Well-Being'. During the twentieth century the men of science gradually became the high priests of our era, their authority was uncontested; they were not even asked to take some equivalent of the Hippocratic Oath. Hiroshima led to the challenging of the divine right of these scientists. But it was really with the advent of the Counter-Culture that scientists began to be dislodged from their pedestals. It was to be revealed that science had encouraged hagiographies of its practitioners and that the great men of science – the Galileos, Keplers, Newtons, Mendels, Pasteurs and Hubbles had been prone to some misdoings. The temples of our time were not to be the laboratories of the men of science, but the Art museums where pictures are hung, in front of which the devotees of Art practise contemplation and meditation. In very much the same way, men and women of the Middle Ages revered the relics of the saints, chasubles or veils, believing that something of the saint continued to live on in them. This parallel has been remarkably analysed by François Duret-Robert in *Marchands d'Art et Faiseurs d'Or* published in 1991.[5] For Duret-Robert, Western society has substituted the religious relic for the work of Art. We believe that in the picture there is something of the personality of the artist and if we are told one day that the picture was not in fact painted by the artist, it ceases to be a relic and we will disregard it. Church relics could be disregarded in the Middle Ages if the ecclesiastical authorities disputed its origin. Duret-Robert also parallels the cult of art with the cult of heroes and ancestors. He recalls that the Spartians stole Oreste's bones because they were convinced that the soul of their hero was in them. And today the Australian aborigines are getting their ancestors' bones back from an Edinburgh museum.

Who decided whether an object is a work of art and deserves veneration? The Art world decides, amateurs and collectors, art historians and critics, museum curators, those who deal in ancient and modern art as well as the artists. And who decides that someone is an artist? The very same, élite group. A peasant or a labourer who declares himself an artist will not be recognised as such unless he penetrates the art circuit. If he heaps up stones in his field and declares this a work of art, he might as well save his breath. On the other hand, a pile of stones in a room in a museum of modern art will be recognised as a work of art in so far as the man who assembled them is recognised as an artist by this élite. Obviously it is easier for a child of the bourgeoisie to be recognised as an artist than a peasant or a labourer because he or she has the chance to rub shoulders with the artistic élite which is (for the most part) bourgeois.

This élite endeavours to distinguish itself from the people by valuing the sort of object, the work of art, which the man in the street cannot recognise as such because he does not know how to decipher its code. Such is the thesis defended by Pierre Bourdieu in his book *La Distinction – Critique sociale du jugement*, in which he shows that the bourgeoisie, unable to rely on the mark of nobility to distinguish itself from the commoner, has gradually created a cultural distinction which puts the man in the street on the defensive. Bourgeois society, in making culture sacred, has excluded from its church the little people who are not initiated into the code we have described above. Bourdieu writes: 'The spectator who is deprived of the specific code feels overwhelmed, "drowned" when confronted by what seems to him a chaos of sound and rhythm, of colours and lines without rhyme or reason.'6

The culture that legitimates these social differences encompasses not only the visual arts but also classical music, opera, ballet, theatre and poetry. Such 'distinction' has been perceived since the nineteenth century by some philosophers, among them Proudhon (quoted earlier) and the Spanish philosopher Ortega Y Gasset, *The Dehumanization of Art* is a clear expression of his ideas, with which Bourdieu agrees in saying that

One might follow Ortega Y Gasset when he attributes to modern art – art which simply follows to its logical conclusion the intention inscribed in art since the Renaissance – a systematic refusal of all that is 'human', meaning the passions, emotions, feelings of *ordinary* men going about their *ordinary* lives, and by the same token all the themes and objects which could arouse them. ... To reject what is 'human' is obviously to reject what is generic, that is, *common*, 'easy' and immediately accessible.7

Ortega Y Gasset goes on to say that this art

compels the average citizen to realise that he is just this – an average citizen, a creature incapable of receiving the sacrament of art, deaf and blind to pure beauty ... which is that art of a privileged aristocracy of finer senses, [and that it] endangers their rights as men ... this new art also helps the élite to recognise themselves and one another in the drab mass of society and to learn their mission, which consists in being the few and holding their own against the many.8

'Modern art,' he maintains, 'is essentially unpopular; moreover, it is anti-popular.'[9] The sociologists of art no longer
make headlines in the journals and art reviews. One of the
greatest art historians, Arnold Hauser, author of *The Social
History of Art*, is almost unknown.

In his book *Art, an Enemy of the People*, Roger L. Taylor
passionately denounced the fact that art created by the bourgeoisie operates against the culturally disinherited.

> As experienced in contemporary society, art is a form of
> life, a conceptual system, which is lived within the bour-
> geois setting. It is from this setting that the art process
> emanates and its life-enhancing ripples do not extend far
> beyond the interests of this social class.[10]
> The 'cultural' life of our society is a confidence trick
> practised on the masses. The masses pay in two ways.
> Firstly, through their pockets in financing the educa-
> tional system etc., which is itself ideologically committed
> to the 'cultural' life, and secondly through a general
> sense of inadequacy (concealed) when measuring
> themselves against the range of skills the social order
> demands.[11]

And he ends by saying that others before him have arrived at
the same conclusion, above all Leo Tolstoy, who wrote *What
Is Art?*

Tolstoy could have called his book 'Against Art and Artists'. In his first chapter, against ballet and opera, he criticises
such cultural manifestations financed by people who sometimes had to sell their only cow in order to pay their taxes. ...
Tolstoy was also indignant over the fact that the monthly
salary of a ballet master was more than the annual wages of
ten labourers. In the same spirit, Jean-Jacques Rousseau had
written that the cheap seats in the theater were proportion-
ately more expensive for the poor than the costly seats for the
rich. And this is even more evidently the case today, when
quite a few theaters are subsidised by the money of those who
cannot afford to attend them. The report *Les Pratiques
culturelles des Français 1973–1989*,[12] financed and published
by the Ministry of Culture and Communications, confirmed

that despite a tenfold increase in subsidies over twenty years, attendance at theatres had decreased. This report confirmed the élitist thesis according to which '"Culture", far from being a neutral thing, is fixed once and for all, serving social groups as a means of distinguishing one from another.'[13] And Augustin Girard, director of the Departement des Etudes et de la Prospective, concluded that 'We should like to prove to the intelligentsia that they are living on a little cloud and that they are attempting to impose on the French a reality which is in fact an élitist reality.'[14] This is not far from Tolstoy's argument in Chapter VIII of *What Is Art?*, where he concludes that it remains the pastime of the rich, not only too costly but also incomprehensible to the majority of the people.

The other theme developed by Tolstoy, which is particularly interesting, is that of the impoverishment of faith in traditional Orthodox religion, which led the Russians of the ruling class to immerse themselves in art as compensation. He does not actually use the word, but he invokes art as a 'spiritual blessing, essential for all men ("like religion", as the devotees of art are fond of saying)'. [15]

In the late twentieth century, Tom Wolfe has brought out the way in which the upper classes in the United States replaced their traditional support for the Church with support for the arts: it is the educated classes' new religion.

It wasn't so long ago that Americans of great wealth routinely gave ten per cent of their income to the church. The practice of tithing was a certification of worthiness on earth and an option on heaven. Today the custom is to give money to the arts. When Mrs E. Parmalee Prentice, daughter of John D. Rockefeller Sr. died in 1962, she did not leave her holdings worth about $5 million to the church. She left them to the Museum of Modern Art for the building of a new wing. ... There was a time not so long ago when American business gave large amounts of money to churches ... it was absolutely necessary. Businesses literally prayed in public. Today what American business would support a religion? Most would look upon such a thing as sheer madness. So what does a corporation do when the time comes to pray in public? It supports the arts … [the Bank of America] hired a curator and began buying works of art at the rate of 1000 a year … [IBM] displayed Michael Heizer's 'Levitated Mass' at its outdoor plaza at Madison Avenue and 56th Street. The piece is a 24-foot-by-10-foot metal tank containing water and a slab of granite.[16]

But what is special about this religion or cult is that it allows you to become wealthy here on earth. The conversion to Art of the American educated set, like that of the European bourgeoisie in recent years, can be explained to a great extent in terms of the desire for profit. The reasoning is not new: in the seventeenth century, as we have seen, the Marquis de Coulanges had advised Madame de Sévigné that pictures were 'as good as gold bars, there has never been a better investment. You will always get double for them if you want to sell.' The mass media, in drawing attention to the phenomenal prices attained in the sales rooms in the late twentieth century, have certainly played a decisive role in the conversion of numerous financiers and businessmen to modern art. Between 1987 and May 1990 prices rose by 100 per cent a year, or more.[17]

What the public and the buyers always seem to disregard is the way that prices are a function of fashion, and that this necessarily changes from one generation to another, from one century to another. While Old Masters have been relatively unprized, modern paintings have been all the rage. But there will be a reversal. We earnestly advise those interested in acquiring works of art to read and reread the works of art historians who have analysed the fluctuations of taste and prices, such as Gerard Reitlinger's *The Economics of Taste – the Rise and Fall of Picture Prices 1760–1960*,[18] and Georges Bernier's *L'Art et l'argent – le marché d'art au XXᵉ siècle*.[19] We learn, for instance, that a Reynolds, *Venus and the Piping Boy*, was sold for £6,770 in 1909, £1,575 in 1928 and only £307 in 1931. Reynolds had been a fashionable painter as Picasso is today. Around the turn of the century, tapestries were as sought after as Van Goghs are today. These days tapestries are not worth a fraction of their price a century ago. Van Gogh certainly had good reason to speak of 'jiggery-pokery over the price of paintings'. A heavy irony in his case, since one of the most famous sales of the decade was that of his *Irises*, auctioned off by Sotheby's in 1987 to the Australian magnate Alan Bond, for £53.9 million, creating a world record for a work of art.

As we entered the 1990s, however, auction prices reached a plateau and even fell. Some public auctions resulted in as much as 50 per cent of their lots unsold. It was not the first or the last time that the art market has experienced price falls. The first example we know of occurred at the end of the fourteenth century, in Avignon, whence the Merchant of Prato wrote to his correspondants in Florence only to buy paintings at reduced prices from the workshops. The popes were about to leave Avignon. We have seen that in seventeenth-century Holland, the economic crisis in the middle of the century led to bankruptcy for Rembrandt and for Vermeer's widow. It is not often noticed that the prices of contemporary works of art collapsed with the French Revolution. Eighteenth-century prices did not recover until more than fifty years later, the Goncourt brothers contributing to their rehabilitation with their book *Les Peintres Français du XVIIIe Siècle*. Later in the century the financial problems of Durand-Ruel lowered the prices of Impressionist paintings for the first time. This was the period in which artists discovered the influence of the stock exchange on their well-being. They discovered this in an even more dramatic fashion in the crisis of 1929. The recollection of that crisis and its consequences for the art market invites us to consider what would happen if there were a new stock market crash. The consequences would be much worse, because in 1929 the United States was still a young nation that could bounce back. Today the United States has aged, and lacks the resources necessary for such a come-back. Such a crash would indeed sound the knell for our civilisation.

The idea that our civilisation could run down and suffer the fate of Greece and Rome is still strange to many in the West.

Each nation, each civilisation, has thought that what happened to others cannot happen to them. Nevertheless, we are showing all the symptoms of a civilisation at the end of its tether: a top-heavy bureaucracy, economic and financial crises, a dramatic fall in population growth, complacency, a decline in traditional civic and moral virtues, a rise in mysticism, science on the defensive, and a decadent art.

Reference notes

1 ☐ Against art and artists

1   Adolf Hitler, *Mein Kampf*, 1925, vol. I, pp. 6–7
2   A. Kubizek, *Young Hitler*, tr. E. V. Anderson, London, 1954, pp. 13–14, 60
3   Hitler, *op. cit.*, vol. I, chap. II, p. 17
4   Thomas Mann, *Gesammelte Werke*, vol. XII, Frankfurt, 1960, pp. 848–9
5   Arnold Hauser, *The Social History of Art*, London, 1951, vol. II, p. 891
6   P.-J. Proudhon, *Du Principe de l'art et de sa destination sociale*, Paris, 1865, pp. 289, 357
7   Jean Gimpel, *The Cathedral Builders*, New York and London, 1961
8   Quoted in Alfred Michiels, *Histoire de la peinture flamande et hollandaise*, Paris, 1847, vol. II, p. 412
9   Montaigne, *Essais*, Livre II, chap. XVI
10 Quoted in Emile Coornaert, *Les Corporations en France avant 1789*, Paris, 1941, p. 131
11 Ambroise Paré, *Oeuvres complètes*, Paris, 1841, vol. II, p. 618
12 François de Hérain, *Peintres et sculpteurs écrivains d'art. De Léonard à Van Gogh*, Paris, 1960, p. 9
13 Georges Mathieu, 'Si ...', *Arts*, no. 861 (21–27 March 1962), p. 1
14 Claude Lévi-Strauss, in an interview with André Parinaud, *Arts, Spécial Picasso*, no. 60 (16–20 November 1966), p. 40
15 Claude Rivière, 'Naissance du monde nouveau', *Iris-Time*, no. 12, 19 February 1964; quoted in Raymonde Moulin, *Le Marché de la peinture en France*, Paris, 1967, pp. 178–9
16 Pierre Restany, 'Monochrome et vitalisme', preface to an exhibition of work by Yves Klein at the Galerie Rive Droite, October 1960; quoted by Raymonde Moulin, *op. cit.*, p. 179
17 Pierre Cabanne, 'Picasso', *Arts, Spécial Picasso*, no. 60, 16–22 November 1966, pp. 12–13
18 Roger Garaudy, *D'un réalisme sans rivages, Picasso, Saint-*

John Perse, Kafka, Paris, 1963, pp. 25–7

19 Julien Benda, *La France byzantine ou le triomphe de la littérature pure*, Paris, 1945, pp. 21, 88, 108, 109, 224, 233, 254

20 Julien Benda, 'Préface' to the new edition of *La Trahison des clercs*, Paris, 1958, p. 20

21 Jean-François Revel, *Pourquoi des philosophes*, Paris, 1957, p. 13

22 Jean-François, Revel, *La Cabale des dévots*, Paris, 1962, pp. 21, 23

2 □ Giotto, the first bourgeois painter

1 Dante, *Purgatorio* XI, lines 94–6, tr. C. H. Sisson, Manchester, 1980

2 J. Gaye, *Carteggio inedito d'artisti dei secoli XIV, XV, XVI*, Florence, 1839, p. 481

3 *Petrarch's Testament*, tr. T. E. Mommsen, Ithaca, N.Y., 1957, pp. 79–81

4 A. Poliziano, *Prose volgari ... e poesie latine*, compiled by Del Lungo, Florence, 1867, p. 156

5 Protocol by Ser Francesco di Boninsegna da Vespignano, 1316–27, c. 119; cf. Baccini, *Messaggero del Mugello*, 12 November 1892, no. 45; quoted in I. B. Supino, *Giotto*, Florence, 1920, p. 318

6 Protocol by Ser Lando d'Ubertino di Compagno da Pesciola, 1318–26, , c. 101; quoted in Supino, *op. cit.*, p. 317

7 Protocol by Ser Lando d'Ubaldino di Compagno da Pesciola, c. 28; cf. Baccini, *Messagero del Mugello*, 18 September 1900, no. 37; quoted in Supino, *op. cit.*, p. 316

8 Cf. Frederick Antal, *Florentine Painting and its Social Background*, London, 1947, p. 160

9 Protocol by Ser Lapo di Ricevuto di Firenze fol. 88 v. (text completed from R. Davidson, *Forschungen zur Geschichte von Florenz*, III, no. 1053, p. 213); quoted in Supino, *op. cit.*, p. 316

10 Quoted in C. Bayet, *Giotto*, Paris, 1907, p. 116

11 The poem has survived in two Mss: Laurent, pl. XC, cod. 47, c. 37h, and Riccard 1717, printed for the first time by C. F. Von Rumohr, *Italienische Forschungen*, 1827, vol. II, pp. 51 ff. (J. Von Schlosser's ed., 1920, pp. 259 ff.)

12 Alexander de Roes, *Memoriale de prerogative imperii Romani*, ed. H. Grundmann Heimpei, *M(onumenta) G(ermanica) H(istorica), Staatschriften des spateren Mittelalters*, vol. I,

no. I, 1958, pp. 94 ff
13 Giovanni Villani, *Cronica*, XI, 12, vol. III, Florence, 1845, p. 232
14 G. Boccaccio, *Il Decameron*, VI, 5
15 Quoted in Bayet, *op. cit.*, p. 143
16 Dante, *Inferno*, XIX, lines 113–14
17 Dante, *Purgatorio* XI, lines 100–2

3 ☐ Towards the Liberal Arts

1 Cennino Cennini, *The Craftsman's Handbook I*, I, Engl. tr. D. V. Thompson Jr., New Haven, Connecticut, 1933
2 Ibid.
3 Ibid., III, LXX
4 Ibid., V, CIV
5 Vitruvius, *The Ten Books of Architecture I*, I, 3
6 Ibid., VI, i, 5
7 Pliny the Elder, *Natural History*, XXXV, 85
8 G. P. Stevens, *The Erechtheum, measured, drawn and restored*, Cambridge, Mass., 1927, pp. 381 ff.
9 Pliny the Elder, *op. cit.*, XXXV, 77
10 Marie Delcourt, *Périclès*, Paris, 1939, p. 173
11 Lorenzo Ghiberti, *Commentarii*, II, 19, ed. J. Von Schlosser, Berlin, 1912
12 Ibid., II, 23
13 L. B. Alberti, *Della Pittura*, III, 2
14 Ibid., I, proem
15 Ibid., II, 7
16 Ibid., II, 6, referring to Pliny the Elder, *Natural History*, XXXV, 135
17 Leonardo da Vinci, *Treatise on painting*, Codex Atlanticus 119, J. P. Richter, *The literary works of Leonardo da Vinci*, 2nd edn., Oxford, 1939, vol. I, p. 116
18 Leonardo, *op. cit.*, Cod. Atl. 117a, Richter, *loc. cit.*
19 Leonardo, op. cit., Codex Urbinas 15v., tr. A. P. McMahon, Princeton, 1956, vol. I, p. 17
20 Ibid., Cod. Urb. 18a, Richter, vol. I, p. 79
21 Ibid., Cod. Urb. 8v, McMahon, vol. I, p. 19
22 Ibid., Cod. Urb. 9z, McMahon, vol. I, p. 19
23 Ibid., Cod. Urb. 20z, 20v, McMahon, vol. I, pp. 35–6
24 Ibid.
25 Marsiglio Ficino, *Opera I*, Basileae 1576, p. 944, letter to Paulus Middleburgensis; quoted in André Chastel, *Marsile Ficin et l'Art*, Geneva and Lille, 1954, p. 61

4 ☐ The Artist is born

1 Georges Renard, *Histoire du travail à Florence*, Paris, 1914, vol. II, pp. 205–6
2 Quoted from Renard, *op. cit.*, vol. II, p. 216
3 Marsiglio Ficino, *Opera I*, Basileae 1576, pp. 296, 298, *Theologia Platonica* XIII, 3
4 Ficino, *op. cit.*, XIII, p. 297, tr. P. Kristeller, *Philosophy of M. Ficino*, New York, 1943, p. 119
5 Ficino, *op. cit.*, X, 4, p. 229
6 (Ed.) L. Beltrami, *Documenti e memorie riguardanti la vita e le opere di Leonardo da Vinci*, Milan, 1919, p. 65, letter to Piero de Nuvolaria
7 (Ed.) J. Gaye, *Carteggio inedito d'artisti dei secoli XIV, XV, XVI, ii*, Florence, 1840, p. 71 Bembo to Isabella d'Este. The translations of Isabella's and Bembo's letters given in R. & M. Wittkower, *Born under Saturn*, London, 1963, pp. 35–6, were consulted.
8 *Vasari's Lives of the Painters etc.*, tr. A. B. Hinds, 4 vols, London & New York (Everyman edn), 1927: 'Andrea del Sarto', 2, p. 311
9 Vasari, 'Leonardo da Vinci', 2, p. 159
10 Vasari, 'Andrea del Sarto', 2, p. 321
11 1 July 1514; tr. R. Friedenthal, *Letters of the Great Artists*, London, 1963, I, p. 45
12 Vasari, 'Bastiano San Gallo', 3, p. 302
13 Vasari, 'Jacopo da Pontormo', 3, p. 250
14 Vasari, 'Michelangnolo Buonarotti', 4, p. 108
15 Benvenuto Cellini, *Vita*, ed. O. Bacci, 1901, pp. 239, 29 ff.; tr. R. H. H. Cust, 1917, II, pp. 81–2
16 Ibid., pp. 11 ff., 143; Cust., I, pp. 278–80

5 ☐ The Church versus the freedom of the artist

1 *Conciliorum oecum, decreta*, cur. J. Alberigo, *et al.*, 1962, pp. 751, 37 ff.
2 Actio VI J. D. Mansi ... *Conciliorum ... collectio*, XIII, 1767, 252
3 Libri Carolini, II, 3, ed. H. Bastgen, *M(onumenta) G(ermanica) H(istorica)*, pp. 98, 21 ff., 100, 9 ff.
4 Ibid., IV, 2, pp. 176, 15 ff.
5 J.-P. Migne, *Patrologica Latina*, CLXXXII, 915 C
6 Ibid., 915 D–916 A
7 Ibid., 916 B

8   Quoted in L. Gillet, *Histoire artistique des ordres mendiants*, Paris, 1912, p. 38, no. I
9   *Statuta generalia* ... ed. M. Bihl, *Archivum Franciscanum Historicum*, XXXIV (1941), 52
10   G. Savonarola, *Prediche sopra Ezechiele*, XLV (XLVI), ed. R. Ridolfi, vol. II, Rome, 1955, pp. 275–6
11   Savonarola, *Prediche italiane ai Fiorentini*, II, ed. F. Cognasso, Perugia, 1930, p. 162
12   Ibid., I, p. 17, 1 November 1494
13   Ibid., ed. R. Palmarocchi, Venice, 1933, p. 391, III, I, 5. III. 1496
14   Wolfgang Stechow, *Northern Renaissance Art (1400–1600)*, ed. H. W. Janson, New Jersey, 1966, pp. 129–30
15   G. Vasari, *La Vita di Michelangelo*, ed. P. Barocchi, vol. I, 1962, p. 75; De Vere IX, 57
16   Michelangelo Buonarotti, *Rime*, ed. E. N. Girardi, 1960, no. 285
17   P. Caliari, *Paolo Veronese*, Rome, 1909, p. 102 ff.
18   G. Paleotti, *Discorso intorno alle imagini sacre e profane*, ii, 35; in P. Barocchi, *Trattati d'arte del Cinquecento*, ii, Bari, 1961, 417
19   E. Mâle, *L'art religieux après le Concile de Trente*, Paris, 1932, p. 111
20   J. Molanus, *De picturis et imaginibus sacris*, ...Lovanii 1570, pp. 65v–66

6 ☐ The artist as civil servant

1   Quoted in *Les Métiers et les corporations de la Ville de Paris*, ed. René de Lespinasse, Paris, 1886, vol. II, p. 206
2   André Félibien des Avaux, *Conférences de l'Académie royale de peinture et de sculpture pendant l'année 1667*, 'Préface', Paris, 1668
3   Pierre Verlet, *Versailles*, Paris, 1961, p. 161
4   Saint-Simon, *Mémoires 1695*, ed. A. De Boislisle, Paris, 1879, vol. II, p. 282
5   Saint-Simon, *Mémoires 1708*, 1902, vol. XVI, pp. 43–4
6   Quoted in Verlet, *op. cit.*, p. 65
7   Quoted in Régine Pernoud, *Histoire de la bourgeoisie en France*, Paris, 1962, vol. II, p. 78
8   Anatole de Montaiglon, *Mémoires pour servir à l'histoire de l'Académie royale de peinture et de sculpture depuis 1648 jusqu'en 1664*, Paris, 1853, Introduction, p. 1

7 ☐ The artist, dealer and critic

1   John Evelyn, *Diary*, ed. E. S. Beer, Oxford, 1955, vol. II, p. 39
2   Quoted in A.-B. de Vries, *Jan Vermeer van Delft*, tr. R. Allen, London, 1948, p. 19
3   'Discours sur les ouvrages des plus excellents peintres anciens et nouveaux ...' Bibliothèque Nationale, Fonds français 16968, col. 124 ff.; this and other extracts published by L. Hourticq, *Gazette des Beaux-Arts*, 1905, 1, p. 327
4   Ibid., p. 327
5   Ibid., MS col. 130, *Gazette des Beaux-Arts*, 1905, 1, p. 333
6   Louis Hourticq, *De Poussin à Watteau*, Paris, 1921, p. 207
7   Quoted in Maurice Rheims, *La Vie étrange des objets*, Paris, 1959, p. 309
8   *Discours ...* Hourticq, quoted in Maurice Rheims, *op. cit.*, pp. 305–6; c.j. *Gazette des Beaux-Arts*, 1905, pp. 247, 331
9   Quoted in Maurice Rheims, *op. cit.*, p. 306
10   Loménie de Brienne, *Memoires*, Paris, 1919, vol. III, p. 90
11   Quoted in Maurice Rheims, *op. cit.*, p. 217
12   *Mémoires inédits sur la vie et les ouvrages des membres de l'Académie royale de peinture et de sculpture*, vol. 1, Paris, 1854, pp. 62–3
13   G. Vasari, *Marc Antonio Bolognese*, Milanesi V, 433, De Vere VI, 114
14   Denis Diderot, *Salon de 1767*, ed. J. Seznec and J. Adhémar, Oxford, 1963, vol. III, p. 53
15   Lafont de Saint-Yenne, *Réflexions*, p. 36; quoted in André Fontaine, *Les Doctrines d'art en France*, Paris, 1909, p. 205
16   Diderot, *Salon de 1765*, vol. II, 1960, p. 76
17   Diderot, *Salon de 1759*, vol. I, 1957, p. 68
18   Diderot, *Salon de 1765*, vol. II, 1960, p. 144
19   Diderot, *Salon de 1763*, vol. I, 1957, p. 222
20   Ibid., p. 223
21   Diderot, *Salon de 1767*, vol. III, 1967, p. 53
22   Quoted in Louis Réau, *Histoire de la peinture française au XVIIIᵉ siècle*, Paris, 1925, p. 39
23   Régine Pernoud, *Histoire de la bourgeoisie en France*, Paris, 1962, vol. II, p. 181
24   Diderot, *Salon de 1767, ed. cit.*, vol. III, 1960, p. 181
25   Edmond et Jules de Goncourt, *L'Art du XVIIIᵉ siècle*, première série, Paris, 1918, p. 380
26   Ibid., p. 344
27   Ibid., p. 344, no. 2
28   Ibid., p. 344–5, no. 2

8 ☐ Towards the religion of the Beautiful

1   Quoted in Louis Hourticq, *De Poussin à Watteau*, Paris, 1921, p. 43
2   Ibid., p. 49
3   Ibid.
4   Roger de Piles, *Cours de peinture par principes*, Paris, 1708, p. 494 ff.
5   Ibid., pp. 489–90
6   Abbé Batteux, *Les Beaux-arts réduits à un même principe*, Paris, 1747

9 ☐ Art for art's sake

1   Alfred de Muset, 'Sonnet au Lecteur', *Poésies nouvelles*, in *Poésies complètes* (Pléiade ed), Paris, 1933, p. 470
2   Alfred ,de Vigny, *Stello* in *Oeuvres complètes* (Pléiade ed), Paris, 1948, vol. 1, p. 793
3   Ibid., p. 800
4   Ibid., chap. XI, p. 802
5   Victor Cousin, *Du Vrai, du Beauet, du Bien*, Paris, 1853, pp. 196–7
6   Théophile Gautier, *Mademoiselle de Maupin*, 'Préface', Paris, 1910, p. 22
7   Théophile Gautier, *L'Artiste*, 14 December 1856
8   Théophile Gautier, *Poésies 1830–1832*, Paris, 1910, vol. I, p. 1
9   Théophile Gautier, *Mademoiselle de Maupin*, p. 22
10   Quoted in Albert Cassagne, *La Théorie de l'art pour l'art en France chez les derniers romantiques et les premiers réalistes*, Paris, 1959, p. 53
11   Ibid., p. 349
12   Ernest Feydeau, *Théophile Gautier, souvenirs intimes*, Paris, 1874, p. 127
13   Cassagne, *op. cit.*, p. 347
14   Gustave Flaubert, *Correspondance*, 2e série (1850–1854), Paris, 1927, p. 286
15   Ibid., p. 129
16   Théodore de Banville, *Commentaire, Odes funambulesques*, Paris, 1833, vol. I, p. 179
17   Sonnet addressed to Ingres; quoted in Louis Hautecoeur, *Littérature et peinture en France du XVIIe au XXe siècle*, Paris 1942, p. 92
18   *Ingres raconté par lui-même et par ses amis,* ed. Pierre Cailler,

Geneva, 1947, vol. I, pp. 41, 45

19 Théophile Silvestre, *Les Artistes français*, Paris, 1926, vol. II, p. 10

20 Quoted in Cassagne, *op. cit.*, p. 101

21 Eugène Delacroix, *Oeuvres Littéraires*, Paris, 1923, vol. I, p. 76

22 Silvestre, *op. cit.*, vol. I, p. 136

23 *Corot raconté par lui-même et par ses amis*, ed. Pierre Cailler, Geneva, 1946, vol. I, p. 97

24 Ibid., p. 90

25 Charles Baudelaire, *L'Art romantique*, XI, Paris, 1954, p. 960

10 ☐ Social art in the service of freedom

1 Gustave Flaubert, *Correspondance*, 3ᵉ série (1854–1869), Paris, 1929, p. 189, letter to Edmond and Jules de Goncourt

2 P.-J. Proudhon, *Du principe de l'art et de sa destination sociale*, Paris, 1865, p. 360

3 F. de Lamennais, *Esquisse d'une philosophie*, Paris, 1840, p. 134

4 Ibid., p. 273

5 Quoted in Albert Cassagne, *La Théorie de l'art pour l'art en France chez les derniers romantiques et les premiers réalistes*, Paris, 1959, p. 49

6 Victor Hugo, *Fonction du poète, les Rayons et les Ombres*, Paris, 1964, vol. I, p. 1025

7 Alphonse de Lamartine, *A Némésis* (Pléiade ed), Paris, 1965, p. 508

8 Lamartine, *Lettre à Guichard de Benassis*, 6 December 1835

9 Louis Hautecoeur, *Littérature et peinture en France du XVIIᵉ au XXᵉ siècle*, Paris, 1942, p. 70

10 Ibid., p. 71

11 Eugène Delacroix, *Journal*, Paris, 1932, vol. II, p. 20, 16 April 1853

12 Quoted in Hautecoeur, *op. cit.*, p. 73

13 Proudhon, *op. cit.*, p. 280

11 ☐ 1839

1 Eugène Delacroix, *Oeuvres Littéraires*, Paris, 1923, vol. I, p. 16

2 Quoted in André Vigneau, *Une brève histoire de l'art de Niepce à nos jours*, Paris, 1963, p. 105

3   Delacroix, vol. I, p. 16
4   Leonardo da Vinci, *Trattato della pittura iii,* Codex Urbinas
    133 r, tr. A. P. McMahon, 433, p. 161
5   MS. D. Institut Fol. 8, translation as in H. and A. Gernsheim,
    The History of Photography ..., London and New York,
    1955, p. 4
6   *Letters of Reynolds,* ed. F. W. Milles, Cambridge, 1929, p. 8,
    4, letter to Burke, 14 August 1781
7   Francesco Algarotti, *Saggio sopra la pittura,* 1763, *An Essay
    on painting,* London, 1764, pp. 64–5
8   Vigneau, *op. cit.,* p. 145
9   Ibid., p. 118
10 Delacroix, *Journal,* Paris, 1932, vol. II, p. 58, 21 May 1853
11 Delacroix, *Oeuvres Littéraires,* vol. I, p. 16
12 Ibid., p. 17
13 Théophile Gautier, *Abécédaire du Salon de 1861*; quoted in
    Aaron Scharf and André Jammes, 'Le réalisme de la
    photographie et la réaction des peintres', *Art de France,* IV,
    Paris, 1964, p. 178
14 Quoted in Aaron Scharf, *Art and photography,* London,
    1968, pp. 127–9
15 Charles Baudelaire, *Curiosités esthétiques,* Paris, p. 771,
    'Salon de 1859'
16 Quoted in Vigneau, *op. cit.,* p. 105
17 Théophile Silvestre, *Les Artistes français,* Paris, 1926, vol. II,
    p. 211
18 Paul Valéry, *Degas, danse, dessin,* Paris, 1960, p. 64
19 Louis Hautecoeur, *Littérature et peinture en France du XVIIe
    au XXe siècle,* Paris, 1942, p. 128
20 Quoted in Aaron Scharf, 'Painting, photography and the im-
    age of movement', *The Burlington Magazine,* London, May
    1962, p. 189
21 Jean Renoir, *Renoir My Father,* London, 1963, p. 161
22 *Manet raconté par lui-même et par ses amis,* ed. Pierre Cailler,
    Geneva, 1953, vol. II, p. 52
23 Quoted in Lionello Venturi, *Les Archives de l'Impressionisme,*
    Paris and New York, 1939, vol. I, p. 49
24 Quoted in Aaron Scharf, *op. cit.,* pp. 127–9
25 Charles Chassé, *Gauguin et son temps,* Paris, 1958, p. 138
26 Eugène Tardieu, 'Paul Gauguin', *Echo de Paris,* 13 May 1895,
    quoted in Bengt Danielsson, *Gauguin in the South Seas,*
    London, 1964, p. 171
27 William C. Seitz, *Monet,* London, 1960, notes on pl. 14
28 Wassily Kandinsky, *Rückblick, 1901–1913,* Berlin, 1913
29 Quoted in Hautecoeur, *op. cit.,* p. 256.

12 □ The artist in the ultimate stage of his evolution

1 P.-J. Proudhon, *Du principe de l'art et de sa destination sociale*, Paris, 1865, pp. 357–60
2 Ibid., I, pp. 2802
3 Emile Zola, *L'Oeuvre*, Paris, 1952, vol. II, p. 91
4 Georges Clemenceau, *Claude Monet, Les Nymphéas*, Paris, 1928, p. 19
5 Sigmund Freud, 'Die Wege der Symptombildung', *Gesammelte Werke XI*, London, 1948, p. 390
6 Freud, *loc. cit*
7 Freud, *op. cit.*, p. 391
8 Ibid., p. 390
9 N. N. Dracoulidès, *Psychanalyse de l'artiste et de son oeuvre*, Geneva, 1952, p. 34
10 Quoted in Arnold Hauser, *The Philosophy of Art History*, London, 1959, p. 55
11 Quoted in Dracoulidès, *op. cit.*, p. 27
12 John Rewald, *Cézanne, sa vie, son oeuvre, son amitié pour Zola*, Paris, 1939, p. 124
13 Ibid., pp. 65–6
14 Ibid., p. 125
15 Ibid., p. 142
16 Ibid.
17 *Lettres de Paul Gauguin à Georges-Daniel de Monfreid*, Paris, 1920, p. 231, letter of 12 December 1898
18 *Lettres de Gauguin à sa femme et à ses amis*, Paris, 1946, p. 284, letter of 15 March 1898
19 *Lettres ... à Monfreid*, p. 170, letter of April 1897
20 Ibid., p. 130, letter of November 1895
21 Ibid., p. 346, letter of October 1902
22 Charles Morice, *Paul Gauguin*, Paris, 1920, p. 58
23 Quoted in Henri Perruchot, *La vie de Gauguin*, Paris, 1961, p. 376
24 *Lettres ... à sa femme et à ses amis,* p. 268, letter of March 1895
25 *Lettres ... à Monfreid*, p. 138, letter of June 1890
26 *Lettres ... à sa femme et à ses amis*, p. 136, letter of October 1888

13 ☐ Modern art: an expression of Western decadence

1 Quoted in John Rewald, *Le Post-Impressionisme de Van Gogh à Gauguin*, Paris, 1961, p. 90
2 Théophile Gautier's introduction to the 1868 posthumous edition of Charles Baudelaire, *Les Fleurs du Mal*, Paris, 1900, p. 26
3 Ibid.
4 Quoted in A. E. Carter, *The Idea of Decadence in French Literature, 1830–1890*, Toronto, 1958, Preface, p. VII
5 Charles Baudelaire, *L'Art romantique*, Paris, p. 1030
6 Charles Baudelaire, *Mon coeur mis à nu*, Paris, p. 1214
7 Charles Baudelaire, *Argument du Livre sur la Belgique*, Paris, p. 1303
8 Charles Baudelaire, *Edgar Poe, sa vie et ses oeuvres*, Paris, 1928, p. 15
9 Charles Baudelaire, *Mon coeur mis à nu*, p. 1213
10 Ibid., p. 1220
11 Charles Baudelaire, *Fusées*, Paris, p. 1201
12 Charles Baudelaire, *Mon coeur mis à nu*, p. 1297
13 Jules Levallois, 'Au pays de Bohème', article in *La revue bleue*, 5 January 1895
14 Quoted in A. E. Carter, *op. cit.*, p. 12
15 Théophile Gautier, Introduction, *Les Fleurs du Mal*, p. 26
16 J.-K. Huysmans, *A rebours*, Paris, 1884
17 G. W. F. Hegel, *Esthétique*, Introd. III, 3, Fr. tr. Charles Bérard, Paris, 1875, p. 18
18 Jean Moréas, 'Le symbolisme', *Figaro littéraire*, Paris, 18 September 1886
19 Paul Verlaine, *L'Art Poétique*, Paris, 1965, p. 326
20 Quoted in Rewald, *op. cit.*, p. 92
21 Stéphane Mallarmé, 'Plainte d'automne', *Vers et Prose*, Paris, 1961, p. 124
22 Quoted in John Rewald, *op. cit.*, p. 300
23 Albert Aurier, *Mercure de France*, December 1892, p. 331
24 Camille Pissarro, *Lettres à son fils Julien*, Paris, 1950, p. 235
25 Quoted in Rewald, *op. cit.*, p. 90
26 Quoted in Hautecoeur, *Littérature et peinture en France du XVIIᵉ au XXᵉ siècle*, Paris, 1942, p. 222
27 Albert Aurier, 'Symbolisme en peinture, Paul Gauguin', *Mercure de France*, March 1891; reprinted in Aurier, *Oeuvres posthumes*, Paris, 1893
28 Maurice Denis, 'Le Salon de la Société des artistes français', *La Dépêche de Toulouse*, 22 and 28 April, and 6 May 1901; reprinted in *Théories, 1890–1910*, Paris, 1913

29 Eugène Delacroix, *Oeuvres littéraires*, Paris, 1923, vol. I, p. 76
30 Maurice Denis, 'A propos de l'exposition d'A. Seguin', *La Plume*, 19 March 1895; reprinted in *Théories, 1890–1910*, Paris, 1913
31 Brassaï, *Conversations avec Picasso*, Paris, 1964, p. 60
32 Charles Baudelaire, *Curiosités esthétiques*, Paris, pp. 907, 908
33 Quoted in A. E. Carter, *op. cit.*, p. 126
34 Charles Chassé, *Les clefs de Mallarmé*, Paris, 1954, p. 29
35 Charles Chassé, 'D'Ubu-roi au Douanier Rousseau', *Nouvelle revue critique*, Paris, 1947, p. 163
36 Charles Chassé, *Gauguin et son temps*, Paris, 1955, p. 49
37 *Lettres de Vincent Van Gogh à son frère Théo*, Paris, 1937 p. 277
38 Quoted in Roland Penrose, *Picasso, his Life and Work*, London, 1958, p. 275
39 Quoted in Anthony Cox, 'Instructive autodestruction', artic in *Art and Artists*, 1966, p. 17

14 □ The religion of Art in the capitalist economy

1 Emile Zola, *L'Oeuvre*, Paris, 1952, vol. I, p. 243
2 Ibid., vol. II, p. 124
3 *Lettres de Vincent Van Gogh à son frère Théo*, pp. 138–9
4 Camille Pissarro, *Letters to his son Lucien*, ed. John Rewald, tr. Lionel Abel, London, 1943, p. 117
   (N.B. in one or two instances the translation has been slightly altered.)
5 Ibid., p. 163
6 Venturi, *Les Archives de l'Impressionisme*, II, p. 170
7 *Lettres de Gauguin à sa femme et à ses amis*, p. 75
8 Ibid., pp. 131–2
9 *Lettres ... à Monfreid*, p. 233
10 *Lettres ... à sa femme et à ses amis*, p. 297
11 Venturi, *op. cit.*, II, p. 188
12 Venturi, II, p. 205
13 Venturi, II, p. 204
14 Venturi, II, p. 156
15 Pissarro, *Letters to his son Lucien*, p. 98
16 Ibid., p. 109
17 Ibid., p. 140
18 Ibid., pp. 208–9
19 Ibid., p. 244

15 ☐ Art: an enemy of the people

1 Emmanuel Todd, *L'Invention de l'Europe*, Paris, 1990, p. 166
2 'L'impatience des croyances de base', *La Vie* 2336 (7–13 June 1990), p. 25
3 Emmanuel Todd, p. 193
4 Ibid., p. 439
5 François Duret-Robert, *Marchands d'Art et Faiseurs d'Or*, Paris, 1991.
6 Pierre Bourdieu, *La Distinction – Critique sociale du jugement*, Paris, 1979, p. 11
7 Ibid., pp. 32–3
8 Ortega Y Gasset, *The Dehumanization of Art*, New York, 1956, p. 6
9 Ibid., p. 5
10 Roger L. Taylor, *Art, an Enemy of the People*, Brighton, 1978, p. 47
11 Ibid., p. 3
12 Olivier Donnat et Denis Coigneau, *Les Pratiques culturelles des Français 1973–1989*, Paris, 1990
13 François Ganon, 'La Culture fout le camp', *Telerama* 2015 (16 May 1990)
14 Ibid.
15 Leo Tolstoy, *What Is Art?*, tr. Aylmer Maude, London, n.d., p. 72
16 Tom Wolfe, 'The Worship of Art – Notes on the new god', *Harpers Magazine*, October 1984
17 Geraldine Norman, 'Fading Images of Wealth', *The Independent* (10 November 1990), p. 39
18 Gerard Reitlinger, *The Economics of Taste – the Rise and Fall of Picture Prices 1760–1960*, London, 1961
19 Georges Bernier, *L'Art et l'argent – le marché de l'art au XXe siècle*, Paris, 1977